D0236309

Not in My Day, Sir

Not in My Day, Sir

Cricket Letters to
The Daily Telegraph

EDITED BY
MARTIN SMITH

First published 2011 by
Aurum Press Limited
7 Greenland Street
London NW1 0ND
www.aurumpress.co.uk

A catalogue record for this book is available from the British Library.

ISBN 978 1 84513 626 0

10 9 8 7 6 5
2015 2014 2013

Typeset by Palimpsest Book Production Limited, Falkirk, Stirlingshire

Printed and bound in Great Britain by MPG Books Ltd, Bodmin, Cornwall

For my sons A.P.J. (bowler) and W.J.J. (batsman), in anticipation of a long, hot, cricket-filled summer

INTRODUCTION

Field marshals, generals, major generals, brigadier generals, brigadiers, colonels, lieutenant colonels, majors, captains, sergeant majors, flight officers: enough top brass to start a fight, if not actually wage the war. Plenty of bluster, too, for this is not the batting order for an Armed Forces XI, but the first battalion of letter writers to *The Daily Telegraph* on the subject of cricket. They are backed up by a legion of reinforcements: the clergy are equally adept with pen and paper, canons to the right, reverends to the left; so too are many a good doctor, MPs, QCs, KTs, OBEs, MBEs, MCCs, and LBWs, not to mention the rank-and-file foot soldiers of the Barmy Army.

The stereotyping that depicts letter writers to the *Telegraph*, and particularly about cricket, as retired colonels from Tunbridge Wells contains more than a grain of truth. They thrive in London and the Home Counties. Over the years there must have been numerous egg-and-bacon-coloured MCC ties splattered with cornflakes after their wearers had choked over their breakfast on the words of E.W. Swanton, Michael Henderson or Simon Hughes.

There is a wonderful moment recalled in Huw Turbervill's *Telegraph* Ashes history, *The Toughest Tour,* when the Duke of Norfolk wakes up one night in 1962 and announces: 'I'd like to manage the tour to Australia,' and his wife responds: 'Well, Marmaduke, you must tell the MCC.' The image can be applied in a blink to a bewhiskered Major Major-type sitting in his MCC monogrammed pyjamas and harrumphing about unshaven players in sunglasses, Twenty20 'whackit' or the ban on taking alcohol into the members' enclosure. To which his wife paraphrases the Duchess of Norfolk: 'Well, darling, you must write to the *Telegraph*.'

And they do, they do. Thankfully they reach for fountain pens rather than double-barrelled shotguns to shoot down Messrs Swanton, Henderson or Hughes metaphorically rather than literally, with the battle cry: 'Have we got any stamps then, dear?' Most days the *Telegraph* postbag contains a sizeable bundle of opinions, diatribes and forceful suggestions about something that has happened on or around one of the world's cricket fields. The best of them may even be published. The very best of them may even appear here.

Anything and everything comes into their sights; a lot of the topics appear again and again like targets on a fairground stall, emphasising that there really is nothing new under the sun when it comes to cricket: the catering is still underwhelming at most grounds, the jobsworth on the gate still over-officious, the selectors always pick the wrong players, and the lbw law remains incomprehensible to all but the legislator who drafted it. And remember it is a *law* rather than a rule, as you will be constantly reminded if you transgress; this is cricket, after all, and rules definitely are not cricket.

If you put together all the theories and suggestions expressed by *Telegraph* readers the result would be a game that resembled a pushmi-pullyu even Dr Dolittle, let alone Dr Grace, would struggle to recognise. If one correspondent had his way, the pitch would look completely different, with the two sets of stumps not aligned: it would prevent bowlers following through, or batsmen running on the line of the stumps, and scuffling up the wicket, he reasoned. Another would have the teams batting alternately from each interval to end the bias of the toss, while in one-day cricket the teams would bat for half their overs, field, then bat and field again to help produce a level playing field. Or should that be an unscuffed wicket? And what is an unlevel playing field, anyway?

However, there would be no Frankenstein's monster if a committee of *Telegraph* readers put together an identikit profile of their perfect player. Far from it. He would wear all-white, never spit, nor chew gum, wear a helmet or have hair longer than is permissible at Sandhurst; nor would he appeal speculatively or speak to the umpire unless spoken to, and he would always salute his superiors, especially if said superior was wearing an MCC tie. A bit of Army discipline never did anybody any harm, old boy.

You wonder how our forefathers got by before the *Telegraph* introduced a daily letters column in the early days of 1928. No doubt a lot of cats, or servants, were kicked before frustration and steaming rages could be channelled into something akin to coherent prose. The column was six or seven weeks old before the first cricket letters were published, and Mr J.A. Milne's proposal for an innovative points-scoring system in the county championship set the tone for the type of borderline-rational ideas that have peppered the pages ever since. (For information, it should be noted at this point that in those inter-War days the domestic fixture list was somewhat haphazard, and counties did not play each other as a matter of course, nor necessarily the strongest opposition, and this was a growing bone of contention.) Proposals for what was euphemistically called 'brighter cricket' were part of the staple diet, and some were certainly colourful.

More than any other sport, cricket appeared with remarkable frequency in the midst of more weighty letter-writing subject matter such as war reparations, the annoying habits of delinquent telegram-deliverers on motorcycles, the rise of Fascism, the non-delivery of parcels from the Antipodes, and how you should handle horses on slippery surfaces.

At times cricket was elevated to such a matter of national importance that it led the letters section. Nowhere was that better illustrated than during the controversy over Bodyline (or Fast Leg Theory, if you prefer) during England's 1932–33 tour to Australia, when a number of bouncers and beamers found their way into the letters column. The d'Oliveira and Packer affairs of 1968 and 1977–78 also raised hackles and the arguments of both sides make interesting reading. Slightly lesser squabbles, such as those centring on Ken Barrington's six-hour century for England against Pakistan, and that over the dirt in Michael Atherton's pocket, also produced lively debate.

In between, there were regular comparisons with the past, great feats, great players, funny turns. Often the writers would drift into an easy-going set of reminiscences, putting each other right, about, say, E.M. Grace, C.B. Fry or Sir Donald Bradman; whether the correct terminology is 'the wicket' or 'the pitch'; and the conundrum of 'why it is that wickets are pitched to start the day's play but stumps are drawn to end it'.

All the best letters columns allow themselves the luxury of witty one-liners and the *Telegraph* has not been slow to follow suit. Some of the best arrived after England's whitewash on the 2006–07 tour to Australia, suggesting the open-topped bus ride that celebrated the long-awaited Ashes success in 2005 be replicated, so that England supporters could boo the disgraced players; failing that, they should be sent home on an open-topped aeroplane.

A personal favourite of the genre, probably because it conjures up images of soccer manager Bill Shankly marking his long-suffering wife's birthday by taking her to a reserve-team game, is from a lady writer: 'When I got married in 1955 my husband told me he was going to give me the greatest thrill a girl could have on her honeymoon; he took me to Lord's.'

Sometimes, though, trawling through mountains of back-copies with ink-encrusted fingers, searching for that nugget of epistolary gold, the excitement of discovery is replaced by a yawning void where an obvious debate should be raging. The lack of comment on Bradman's farewell flailing of the Poms in 1948 can be partly explained away by the shortage of news-print in those post-War years; but surely the colonels in the shires spluttered with indignation at, say, the introduction of helmets in the Seventies, or when the participants in a one-day game were revealed to be bona fide cricketers rather than the cast from a production of Lloyd Webber and Rice's *Joseph and the Amazing Technicolor Dreamcoat.* As an historian you long to hear contemporaneous public opinion on such hot topics; maybe, though, they failed to ignite the imagination, or did not fit in with the editor's agenda that day.

It was not until the arrival of stand-alone supplements in the early Nineties, and the subsequent extra space created, that letters started appearing in the sports section, initially on a Monday and thereafter on various days in midweek. Now cricket had to fight its corner against soccer and myriad other sports, but having held its own against all-comers on the news pages it wasn't about to concede a column inch. Cricket letters continue to appear in *both* sections, unlike most of its sporting rivals, with the notable exception of tennis.

Nowadays missives also come in the form of emails, or as entries on comment walls. More's the pity. Too often the 'send' button on the screen is hit without the built-in time-delay for reflection that finding writing paper, a pen that works, an envelope, a first-class stamp, plus the leisurely walk to the postbox, would bring. There used to be scope for second thoughts, and another screwed-up ball of paper winging its way towards the wastepaper bin in the manner of a return from Jonty Rhodes.

The modern-day means of communication enable anyone with access to a computer the opportunity to sound off behind *noms de plume* like ashes2005, brucexxxx or howzat501 without having to take personal responsibility for their witterings. True, correspondents in the Twenties and Thirties were able to hide behind pseudonyms like 'Cricketer', 'Spectator', 'First Wicket', 'Bat – Not Leg' and 'Common-sense', but this practice was soon stopped. An address, not an anonymous 'via email', should always be a prerequisite, even if it is only a rough geographical area. It provides an idea of why the writer has come down on a particular side in a discussion about where the blame lies for, say, a famous run-out in the late Seventies. You would expect T. Kyte of Yorkshire to be defending Geoff Boycott, and T. Bridge of Nottingham standing foursquare with Derek Randall, but you might wonder about the motivation of I. Botham from Taunton. As one correspondent admitted: 'Much of the enjoyment of the letters page comes from connecting what they say with where they come from.'

Hopefully that enjoyment, and many others besides, will continue when dipping in and out of this compilation, whether you are a military man or a lady promised something special on her honeymoon. The letters in this selection appear chronologically, apart from where it makes sense not to interrupt the flow of a theme or argument, and individual letter headings are as they originally appeared.

If you feel sufficiently moved to respond to any of the issues raised within these pages, please be aware that the correspondence on these topics has now closed, for some as long as eighty years ago.

This book would not have been possible without the help and expertise of a number of people. Consequently, my thanks must go, initially, to Graham Coster for commissioning this collection on behalf of Aurum Press; to Caroline Buckland, Head of Books and Entertainment at Telegraph Media Group, for helping to push the project through; to Aurum – particularly my hard-working editor, Barbara Phelan – for publishing it; to the unbelievably helpful Gavin Fuller, Lorraine Goodspeed and the rest of the staff in the *Telegraph* library for facilitating the research; to my trusted former colleague

Andrew Baker for making the right noises at the right time; to the editors who, over the years, have selected and published the letters; and, most importantly, to the unsung battalions out there who were sufficiently moved to put a stamp on the envelope. I salute you.

MARTIN SMITH
February 2011

PREFACE

BATTLE LINES DRAWN ACROSS THE WICKET

SIR – I feel it would be quite informative if in future you printed the age of the letter-writer alongside their name. I say this because I'm sick and tired of reading letters from English cricket supporters whinging on about shaving, baseball caps, sunglasses, tucking your shirt in, not smiling enough, being aggressive and gesturing at dismissed batsmen by bowlers (Dominic Cork being regularly cited), etc.

The people who write complaining of such matters surely come from the 'Not in my day' generation of the over-fifties. When will they realise that cricket is about winning? Personally, I wouldn't care if Mike Atherton took to the field with a W.G. Grace-size beard, wearing a dressing-gown and goggles, with a fag hanging out of the corner of his mouth and swearing like a trooper, if it meant a winning England team.

D.M. Hamsworth
(Aged 29)
Brighton

DEAR SIR

22 FEBRUARY 1928

CRICKET CHAMPIONSHIP

SIR – I read with great interest the article in today's issue of *The Daily Telegraph* on the county championship. You rightly state that what is required is a scheme to translate automatically the result of the season's cricket into an order of merit. I submit that the following scheme will achieve this, and will also encourage brighter and sporting cricket by inducing teams to go all out for a win. It gives full credit for the batting, bowling, and fielding ability of each team as shown by actual cricket played; for even if a match be so interfered with by rain that only two hours' play is possible, the cricket result of those two hours of play can be duly incorporated in the championship table, and bears its small part in determining the 'order of merit' for the season.

The real cricketing merit of a team must depend obviously upon: a) its ability to score runs (batting), and b) its ability to get its opponents out as cheaply as possible (bowling, fielding, and wicketkeeping). To reflect these abilities accurately can only be done on a basis of runs scored per wicket fallen, for and against, throughout the season. By contrasting one with the other we get an accurate guide to the real cricketing merit of each team, apart from the fortuitous winning or losing of games played. The following example shows the practical working of the scheme:

	Total Runs Scored	Total Wickets Fallen	Average per Wicket	Net 'Merit' of Team
Ayrshire	9,000	300	30	
Opponents	7,750	310	25	5
Banffshire	10,500	300	35	
Opponents	9,760	305	32	3

I claim that the above 'championship table' accurately reflects the actual respective abilities of the Ayrshire and Banffshire teams (batting, bowling, and fielding), based on the cricket actually played.

To provide an effective incentive to win (and thus give brighter cricket), I would credit ¼ run to the 'net merit of team' for each win, as compensation and reward for the risks taken in the sporting attempt to force a win. Assuming Ayrshire to have won 16 matches and Banffshire 12, the 'championship table' would be completed as follows:

	Net Merit of Team	No of Wins	Championship Merit
Ayrshire	5	16	9 (5+4)
Banffshire	3	12	6 (3+3)

It will be objected that the scheme is too complicated and 'mathematical'. Even if this be true, it is worth it if it solves the championship difficulty and does justice to the teams who play for it. And, after all, the only persons affected by the 'complications' and 'mathematics' are the sports editors of our newspapers, who are in a hopeless minority compared with the cricket-loving public! And minorities must suffer!

J.A. Milne
Palmer's Green

4 JULY 1928

A SUGGESTED REMEDY

SIR – Everybody sings out about the vanishing liveliness of the cricket of today, yet all seem to 'funk' making any attempt to get it back.

All recognise that the perfect grounds etc have practically done away with the chance of what is known in golf as 'a rub of the green' ever affecting results in cricket nowadays, and the effect is to make the defence less difficult, and the attack more difficult than of old. In other words, increased powers of endurance are required in the bowler and less in the batsman, so that the batsman gets more and the bowler less than his true cricket value reflected in the scores.

One practical remedy suggested is that, as a fair compensation to the bowler for his loss of the element of chance in leading the attack, his maiden overs should be scored against the batsman (say by the forfeit of two runs) just as his no-balls and wides are scored against the side fielding. Surely it is the kind of suggestion worth experimenting with and without delay, e.g. in the next Gentlemen versus Players match.

It would give due recognition to masterly bowling more certainly than the actual fall of wickets by itself at present can do. It would severely discount 'stonewalling' and do something to redress the unsporting inequality of the contest between bowler and batsman that these magnificent grounds have unwittingly engendered.

Also, it would considerably add to the fun to know that at the end of a season a batsman's average might possibly work out as an average loss to his side of (say) twenty runs every innings he played for them.

Paulet S. Mildmay
Cowes

10 JULY 1928

BRIGHTENING CRICKET

SIR – The remedy for slow cricket, without altering the size of bat, ball, or stumps, or in any way revolutionising the game, is one that I have for years suggested to the MCC.

The change is merely to add to the rules: 'That any batsman who, having been at the wickets one completed hour, has not scored thirty runs, shall be out – time retired.'

H.F. Harrison
Maidstone

11 JULY 1928

'LEAVE THE RULES ALONE'

SIR – Does Mr H.F. Harrison expect his letter to be taken seriously with reference to an alteration of rules, as to a time limit for a batsman's innings?

A good example can be found in the Yorkshire versus Surrey match, at Bradford, yesterday. Surrey had then lost five wickets for 96. Mr Jardine comes in and is joined by Mr Fender, and managed to play out the rest of the day. I noticed that Mr Jardine took two and a half hours to complete his 50, but on the other hand, Mr Fender was scoring at nearly double the pace. Had Mr Jardine had to retire after the first hour in not completing his 30 runs, as suggested by Mr Harrison, what prospect would Surrey have had in making any fight against a powerful side like Yorkshire?

If this suggested rule were incorporated in the Rules of Cricket, many other startling things might happen. Suppose, for instance, No. 1 batsman had got well set and his side required 100 runs to win when he was joined by the last man. He would naturally try and score one run off the last ball of each over, so as to get the next over. His colleague at the other end might not get five or six overs the whole of his innings, and would only try to keep his end up while No. 1 did the scoring. Would No. 11 batsman be compelled to retire for not scoring 30 runs in an hour?

The whole thing seems absurd.

Edwin W. Shepherd
187 Piccadilly W1

26 MARCH 1929

SAFETY FIRST OR THE MATCH-WINNING SPIRIT

SIR – 'Safety first' is a maxim which in ordinary life one can carry too far, for otherwise real deeds of derring-do, which one thrills to hear of and delights to see, would belong to the past. But there can be no doubt whatsoever that no true sportsman ever even dreams of playing for safety. It is for him victory or defeat.

May I tell a story? I was a member of the club who first won a challenge cup competed for by London suburban clubs. Early in its career there had been a captain who, on being asked to accept the office, remarked: 'I only do so on the understanding that for the coming season I have the absolute right of choosing the team to play from week to week.' It was agreed. 'Then,' said he, 'woe to the chap who plays for his own hand, I shall not care whether he is the cleverest bowler or the finest bat. Out he goes! If having first innings, the time has arrived, as I may think, when, if we are to have a chance of winning, we must cut our innings short, every man still to bat will be ordered to have a go at every ball in order to give the other fellows time to win if they are good enough.'

Never was there such a captain. He sought only to make matches with the strongest clubs, and never accepted a challenge from a weak one. Nevertheless, except when rain interfered, no draw ever appeared in our scoring book for two seasons, nor did we have to record a loss.

Henry Williams
Shanklin

13 AUGUST 1929

WHEN IS A WICKET DOWN?

SIR – Having been away from home I am only now able to comment on an incident in the Kent versus Lancashire match at Maidstone on Friday, 26 July. From the description of Friday's play in your issue of Saturday, 27 July, it appears that B.H. Valentine, of Kent, was given out 'bowled' when one bail had merely been moved from its groove without falling.

Surely Law 21 requires a bail to be 'struck off'? A special reference is made (in the 1929 rules, at least, as given in *Wisden*) to the preceding law, which gives this as a condition necessary for the wicket being regarded as 'down'.

I should like to read what more expert readers think on this question.

A.M. Robertson
Beddington

16 AUGUST 1929

MIDDLE STUMP OUT BUT BAILS UNDISTURBED

SIR – Some of your readers may be interested in the following curious incident which occurred in a cricket match last Saturday (10 August) between two Berkshire villages, Hagbourne and Didcot.

One of the Hagbourne batsmen was bowled, his middle stump being knocked out of the ground. The bails, however, did not move, and by some curious chance remained in their original position supported merely by the two outside stumps. According to Law 20 of the Laws of Cricket it seems as if the wicket was not down, and that therefore the batsman was not out, but it is a nice point.

H.A. Smith-Masters
Vicar of Hagbourne

3 JULY 1930

BATSMAN AND BOWLER

SIR – May I suggest that the reason the bat now dominates the ball in cricket is that the silly idea that it is bad form to pull a ball to leg is dead.

When 50 years ago I was being taught to play cricket I was fearfully frowned on when I pulled a ball to leg. In vain I urged that one went in to make runs, and not to worship Mrs Grundy.

Roger Hall
London SE19

13 AUGUST 1930

IS GRACE SURPASSED?

SIR – As an old lover of cricket, I cannot see how Hobbs can ever be in the same street at cricket as such veterans as W.G. Grace, W. Rhodes, G.H. Hirst, and a few other all-round cricketers.

W.G.'s record in first-class matches reads 54,896 runs, 2,876 wickets. Rhodes and Hirst have similar all-round records. Records like these take some surpassing: 1896, W.G. Grace, 2,622 runs, 129 wickets; 1906, G.H. Hirst, 2,385 runs, 208 wickets; 1909, W. Rhodes, 2,094 runs, 141 wickets; and these three played cricket for years like this.

In 1895, W.G. Grace made his 1,000 runs in ten innings (1,016), averaging 112.88. For MCC, W.G. on one occasion took all ten wickets and scored 104 in an innings. On another he took 17 wickets in the match, Gloucestershire versus Notts, for 89 runs.

H.A. Cowell
North Finchley

19 AUGUST 1930
THE UMPIRES' THIRST

SIR – You have probably received innumerable letters, relevant and otherwise, on the subject of the Test match. May I, however, bring one small point to your notice.

During the course of play on Saturday the players received refreshment on several occasions, and deservedly so. I was, however, surprised to notice that no drink was offered to the umpires. Surely their work must be thoroughly exhausting, and they should, like anybody else, be supplied with refreshment.

J.F. Hammond
Cambridge

29 AUGUST 1930
RECALLING THE GOLDEN AGE

SIR – The golden age of English cricket as I remember it was from about 1840 (vide *Tom Brown's School Days*) to 1880. Later the billiard-table grounds upset the balance between bowler and batsman, so that the Laws had to be revised again and again, sanctioning round-arms and then over-arm bowling and so on. I suggest that with our grounds as they now are we want laws such as these:

Not more than ten minutes may lapse between the fall of one wicket and that of the next, or in default of this the retirement of that batsman who has been batting longest.

Matches shall be one-day fixtures in general, play beginning at eleven and concluding at seven, a luncheon interval between one and two alone interrupting the game.

The game shall not be interrupted for rain, nor for bad light, but where the umpires on appeal agree that the light is defective, the bowler may bowl underhand only.

For specially important matches the game shall extend to two days, and the time that two batsmen may continue together at the wicket shall then be 20 minutes.

These laws may make the game something like I remember it, when English cricket was played, not the imitation that has injured its name.

Peter Mondfort
London EC4

AN EXCITING TIE

SIR – Apropos the tie between the Australians and Gloucestershire, your cricket correspondent truly remarks that these rarely occur. I have one in my memory which you may think worth relating. The match was between Surrey and Middlesex, and the counties being neighbours, it was the 'needle match' of the year.

Surrey were batting, and when the last two men were in they needed two runs to tie and three to win. The last ball of an over had arrived, and from this Barratt, a good and safe batsman, made a run which could easily have been converted into a two. But Barratt declined to run the second, and for good reason.

His *vis-à-vis* was a fine bowler; but, if he did, in fact, possess any batting skill, he kept it well within his own ken. Therefore Barratt felt that, as a tie was no earthly use to Surrey, and as he had a fair chance of making the winning hit out of one of the five balls coming to him, he would 'have a go'. Alas, the 'go' resulted in his being bowled neck and crop by the first ball of the five.

Jubilation on the part of the supporters of Middlesex was somewhat damped, however, later on, when it was notified that Surrey in the early part of the last innings had not been credited with a run one of its players had made. The result after all was a tie.

Henry Williams
London NW11

5 SEPTEMBER 1930
ENCOURAGING RUNS FOR SINGLES

SIR – May I express my belief that an effective remedy for dull cricket must provide an incentive which will be felt at the wicket as each ball is sent down?

I would suggest that an extra be added to the total for every ball scored off, and one deducted for every ball not scored off, the extras to be added or deducted at the end of each over to avoid the complication of including them in the individual batsmen's scores.

The scoring of a single or a two more often than not engages half the side in an attempt to field the ball or back up the throw-in, to the obvious advantage of players and spectators alike, whereas a loose ball, hit for four, on a present-day ground surface, frequently gives the field no time even to move, and its whereabouts only becomes apparent to spectators at ground level when one of their number throws it in from the ropes.

Captain W.A. Powell
Andover

18 JANUARY 1933

TEST MATCH TACTICS

SIR – 'Bitterness and acrimony have marked the Test match, which is one of the most unpleasant on record, both on and off the field' – thus the cable reads.

So serious are Test match episodes becoming, and so frequent, that it may be in the best interests of Anglo-Australian friendship to discontinue them. There are more important things than cricket.

This unfortunate tendency is largely due to the ability of the bowler to injure and intimidate the batsmen by bowling at them rather than at the wicket. That, at least, is the contention of many. For this reason we could well adopt a rule from baseball. In that game when the striker is struck by the pitcher he is given a free base. This in baseball is a very great concession.

If in cricket the umpire were empowered to award from one to ten runs to the side on which a batsman was struck by the bowler, many of these unpleasant episodes would be avoided, and there would be a direct incentive to the bowler to avoid hitting the batsman.

W. de Burgh Whyte
London SW1

19 JANUARY 1933

FOR BATSMEN TO SETTLE

SIR – Some of us who have seen Stoddart, 'Ranji', and J.T. Brown hook Kortright and Lockwood off their eyebrows will be wondering what all the present bother is about. If Woodfull and Oldfield, who are approaching middle-age, are too slow to deal with the fastest bowler in the world in like manner they should step back and allow the ball to go to the wicket-keeper.

W.E. Wilkins
Henley-on-Thames

21 JANUARY 1933
INCIDENTS IN 1896 MATCH

SIR – In 1896 in the first match at Sheffield Park of the tour of the ninth Australian team there was a memorable stand made by Dr W.G. Grace and F.S. Jackson. Both stood up to the bowling, and hooked Jones's fastest deliveries however near they happened to go to their heads. They were both much knocked about, and F.S. Jackson was actually found on the completion of his innings to have a broken rib!

I do not recall, however, that any protests were made, or that 'W.G.' threatened to withdraw from the captaincy of the England team, although many cricketers had grave doubts as to the fairness of Jones's bowling action, and he was actually no-balled some years later by the English umpire, Jem Phillips, for throwing!

I think it is useful to recall these facts at the present juncture in view of the outcry in the Australian press about the English fast bowlers.

W.H. Peregrine Adams
Golders Green

BATSMEN'S 'SQUEALING'

SIR – 'Bad workmen find fault with their tools.' Messrs Wood-full, Bradman and Co., being unable to find any defects in their bats, have to look elsewhere for excuses for their many recent failures, and so attack our fast bowlers. I venture to say that if the above-named had piled up runs against us during the present tour, as they have been known to do hitherto, one would have heard little or nothing of the accidental knocks some of the Australians have received.

These knocks are no worse, and probably less severe, than some of those received by certain of our leading batsmen from the hands of Gregory and Macdonald – knocks which produced no squealing on our side then.

H.C.P. Wood
Junior Carlton Club

23 JANUARY 1933

W.G. GRACE'S PUNISHMENT

SIR – In 1896 W.G. Grace had six or seven huge black marks all round the heart region, received from the bowling of Ernest Jones. But did we hear any whine from him about it? Not a word. Neither, in earlier days, did we complain of Spofforth, the 'demon bowler'.

H.K. Fox
Nottingham

THE LOSS OF AN EYE

SIR – I am under the impression that Bates, an English professional, lost an eye in Australia while playing for a team of professionals that toured in Australia in the winter of 1884–85. I cannot now recollect the exact circumstances, but it was impressed on my memory by the fact that I played in a XXII of Suez in a friendly match against the XI of pros going to Australia, and sat next to Bates at lunch.

Lieutenant-Colonel Herbert W.L. Holman
Hove

'PENALTY' RUNS

SIR – I am much intrigued by Mr W. de Burgh Whyte's suggestion that, to avoid unpleasant episodes, the umpire should
have power to award up to ten runs to the side on which a
batsman was struck by the bowler. I venture to suggest some
further advantages of his scheme:

1) The unpleasant episode of a batsman being given out lbw
would be avoided;

2) It would lead to faster scoring and, therefore, to 'brighter
cricket', for even the slowest batsman, with the aid of a sympa-
thetic umpire, could score at the rate of sixty runs an over off
the deadliest spin bowling on the trickiest of wickets;

3) It would save the batsman the expense of buying a bat
and the fatigue of carrying one.

P.T. Baker
Rochester

'SAFETY FIRST' SPORT

SIR – Is not the trouble about 'bodyline' bowling typical of this
'Safety First' age? There have been ten times more players
injured by tackling in Rugby football than by fast bowling in
cricket, but no one proposes to stop tackling.

H.G. Watkins
Hampshire

THE NAVY'S WAY

SIR – I was playing some years ago in a village cricket match at
Selsey. Our opposing team was composed of naval officers and
men. Visiting teams occasionally called our wicket dangerous.
We preferred to call it 'sporting'.

The first ball of the match got up sharply and laid out the

burly sailor who was batting. He was compelled to retire. After a few more wickets had fallen he came back to resume his innings, to the applause of the audience. Our 'demon' bowler was still bowling. To the horror of us all his next ball did precisely the same as his first and caught the gallant fellow with a loud smack on the side of the face; this time not quite so severely as the original blow.

He walked straight to square-leg umpire – we thought to protest. Nothing of the kind! He simply took out his false teeth and asked the umpire to hold them while he continued his innings. By King's Regulations his false teeth were the property of H.M. Government, who had supplied them. His body was his own!

Charles L. Nordon
London EC2

25 JANUARY 1933
THE PERFECT CURE!

SIR – Mr P.T. Baker hurls derision at my suggestion that a bowler should be penalised for deliberately bowling at the batsman.

He suggests that the batsman, in collusion with the umpire, could amass runs by intercepting the ball with his body. A sufficiently thick-headed batsman by repeatedly stopping Larwood with his head might make more runs than by the use of his bat. The coroner could then count the bumps on his head and check the score.

There may be others sufficiently thick-headed to put such a construction on my suggestion. Properly applied it would cure body-bowling.

W. de Burgh Whyte
Conservative Club
London SW1

27 JANUARY 1933

SPORT IN ITS TRUE PLACE

SIR – I am heartily sick of the controversy regarding bodyline bowling in the Test matches. To my mind, cricket ends where it begins – on the field – and the umpires should be competent to give the first and the last word.

I have no time for a sport which is likely to cause bad feeling between nations. Sport, as I understand it, is relaxation which should fit us the better for earning our daily bread, and if relaxation as such is to be made a business, then the sooner we have finished with it the better.

A great deal of our trouble is due to the fact that we are trying to do the impossible – mix work and play together.

Charles E.A. Howard
Radlett

31 JANUARY 1933

CRICKET IN A PLAY

SIR – May I first record my thanks for your critic's warmly appreciative notice of *Mother of Pearl* at the Gaiety, and my gratification that the play, and in particular Madame Delysia's brilliant performance have won such glowing tributes throughout the Press? And then may I say a word in defence of my friend, Mr A.P. Herbert, the author, who is too modest to champion himself?

Mr Darlington deplores a reference to Australian cricket, saying, 'Whatever anybody's views on the leg-theory may be, it is in very bad taste.'

The libretto of *Mother of Pearl* was completed, and the character of the cricketer conceived, many weeks before the Test season began, and it is only an accident that has given to this particular line the appearance of a topical gag. Long before the 'leg-theory' discussions began to be carried on so heatedly (often by laymen who have never had a cricket ball in their hands), this line was written with quite a different idea behind it.

When the young cricketer makes ardent love to Pavani, and she asks, 'Is this cricket?' he replies, 'Yes, Australian rules', but the reference is to the world-famous reputation of the Australian for gallantry with the ladies. There is no attempt at scoring a laugh off the problems which are now weighing down the Test committees.

Chas B. Cochran
London W1

Mr W.A. Darlington writes: Mr Cochran's courteous letter relieves my mind. I had thought it very strange that Mr A.P. Herbert should seem to have been guilty of an error of taste. It is now clear that he was not.

But Mr Cochran's memory is at fault on a small but important point. It is not the famous amorist Pavani to whom the cricketer is making love when the sentence in question is spoken, but Pearl – the wife of his best friend. Consequently when she asks, 'Is this cricket?' and he replies, 'Yes – Australian rules', it sounds as though an insinuation against Australian fair play is intended.

Since the Test match squabble has been magnified to such ridiculous proportions of late, I still feel that the remark will never now be understood in the sense in which Mr Herbert wrote it, and therefore had better be omitted.

7 JUNE 1934

THE GLUT OF RUNS

SIR – I was much interested in Mr Campbell's letter on present-day cricket. I recently watched four days' cricket on the

Taunton ground. During that time about 2,000 runs were scored, including eight separate centuries and two scores over 90.

I was sitting next to one of the most distinguished of our elder 'cricket' statesmen and he said to me: 'I cannot think why people come to see this sort of thing. Unless something is done to help the bowler first-class cricket will become a farce.'

When a wicket is so good that it will not take 'spin' or 'bite', what is a bowler to do against a strong batting side who take no risks? Even when a ball beats the bat there are generally a pair of stout pads in the way, and umpires seem to have a curious reluctance to give a man out lbw.

No wonder our fast bowlers break down under the strain. On the other hand, when the wicket does help the bowler, the batsman has become so pampered that he cannot make runs.

Craufurd Hutchinson
Taunton

8 JUNE 1934

THIS GLUT OF RUNS

SIR – Are we never to be satisfied? During the last year or two we have heard so many complaints about the dullness of cricket, the uninteresting and painful stonewalling, and the general 'decline' of our national game.

Now when there is – as your correspondent terms it – a 'glut' of superb batting and quick scoring, and, as a result, some high totals, we still hear complaints – this time that the bowlers are not getting a chance.

May I point out that it is not the professional mastery of the ball and defensive methods of play that are the cause of these high scores, but rather the state of the ground, and hence the wickets upon which these matches are played.

It was a well-known fact that a hard wicket is the batsman's paradise. Why then should the batsman who is proficient enough to seize the scoring possibilities on present-day wickets be saddled with accusations that he is playing a 'defensive' innings?

We cannot have it both ways. If the wicket is soft and tricky there are more likely to be bowlers' harvests, but while these hard, true wickets last we shall keep hearing of huge totals being scored by men who are brightening cricket.

To make 200 runs without flaw or mistake can hardly be called dull and farcical. What shall we say when there is a row of 'ducks' on the list, and bowlers have come into their own again? I suppose we shall forget these batting heydays, and yearn in our discontented way for the 'Graces and Trumpers of the good old days', maintaining that our cricketers are once more ruining the game by their dull and lifeless methods!

Undeviginti
Reading

11 JUNE 1934
'W.G.'S' BAT

SIR – May I remind your correspondent Mr Duff Tollemache that the famous bowler, Emmett, speaking of the great 'W.G.', said: 'I call him a nonesuch; he ought to be made to use a littler bat.' This remark was made somewhere about 1878, so it appears that the 'littler bat' plea is of very long standing indeed.

Hillite
Twickenham

KNOCKING THE BOWLER 'OFF'

SIR – Years ago I watched Humphreys, of Sussex, hopelessly tying up and skittling out the best Somerset bats with his extremely slow and wily lobs.

Then J.B. Challen came in, threw discretion and orthodoxy to the winds, took the long handle, danced yards down the pitch, and so belaboured Humphreys that he had perforce to be taken off – 52 runs (if I remember correctly) being scored in three overs.

Would it not be worth while for some enterprising county side (say Kent) thoroughly and courageously to try out this method?

T.G. Powell
Ipswich

SHIFTING THE FIELDSMEN

SIR – In order to conciliate the Australians, we are not to allow the bunching of fieldsmen on the leg side by fast bowlers. It therefore seems reasonable that there should be a limit to the closeness by which the Australians may approach the bat when Grimmett or any other slow bowler is bowling.

The batsman knows that the only way to move the fieldsman is to wait for the loose ball and then deliberately take aim, hoping to 'score a bull'. It is not quite cricket, for in the mind of the batsman there is always the irritating feeling that while he does not wish to injure, he must remove the man.

In most cases this unlimited 'in-fielding' amounts to obstruction, and is just as likely to injure a fieldsman as fast bowling to a leg field is likely to injure a batsman.

E.G. Bisseker
London W1

20 JUNE 1934

LARWOOD'S VICTIMS

SIR – The MCC in their cable to the Australian Board of Control on 14 June 1933, stated:

'Bowling on the leg stump with the field placed on the leg side necessary for such bowling is legitimate and has been in force for many years. It is generally referred to as leg-theory.'

I was in Australia during the last visit of the English team, and was present during some of the Test matches. In my opinion neither the so-called 'bodyline' bowling nor any other 'theory' was responsible for the Australian batsmen's downfall. It was Larwood's accuracy and pace that beat them, whether the deliveries were on the leg or the off side. This was proved by the fact that a big percentage of the wickets captured by Larwood were clean bowled.

Observer
Devonshire Club
London SW1

29 JUNE 1934

TRAFFIC IN TEST MATCH TICKETS

SIR – Two friends of mine visited Lord's last Monday, arriving after the gates were closed. They were approached by a newsvendor, who offered them eight shilling and six penny stand tickets for 25 shillings each. They endeavoured to bargain, but were informed: 'It is all right; the way the game is going, I'll get two guineas each for them at lunch-time.'

I regret to say they each paid the 25 shillings. Are the MCC aware of the extent of this trafficking, and, if so, what are they doing about it?

Fairplay
London NW7

26 AUGUST 1938

FUTURE OF TEST MATCHES

SIR – The Oval Test may have been farcical but it was the kind of cricket forced on us by our Australian rivals, only this time we played it better.

England made 903 for seven, not only because of the state of the wicket – there was also the extreme poverty of Australia's attack. If the Australians had won the toss it is unlikely that they would have made anything like our score. Our bowling is superior to theirs, and the average run-getting capacity of our first seven batsmen is decidedly better.

Our batsmen showed fine discipline in continuing to play the right kind of game in the particular circumstances, and it seems unfair that their performance should be overshadowed by reflections about the evil of 'timeless' Tests.

Robert Herrmann
London W2

29 AUGUST 1938

TEST CRICKET FUTURE

SIR – It is to be hoped that the farce at the Oval will kill the 'timeless' Test match in this country, though there are many who say that what is mischievous is not the time factor but the over-preparation of wickets.

But may one point out to those who consider every unfinished match a 'wash-out' that to draw a game – better say to 'save' the game – against heavy odds has always been one heroic feature of cricket; and while no one wants a whole series of drawn matches between England and Australia, to legislate in such a way as to make a drawn game impossible would rob the game of one of its glories.

Cricket, as we have known it in the past, has not only been

a game between two elevens, but a game played also against the clock and the weather; and it is the time factor (plus the weather) which causes so much of the drama and evokes the highest strategic skill and personal sacrifice.

It has always seemed strange to me that whereas many county matches are finished in three days, it is assumed that international matches cannot be finished in four. Surely if there is a higher standard of batting in Test matches, there should also be a higher standard of bowling. We ought not to make it too easy for 'robots' to win anyhow.

No doubt many would like to see every Test played to a finish, with choice of first innings awarded to each team alternately. But I think it well that we should retain some of those features which, in the past, have contributed to the fun of the game.

Dr Leonard Inkster
Newton St Cyres

SIR – Are not some of the commentators losing their heads? That England made a magnificent score at the Oval is no proof that the wicket was 'impossible' from the bowlers' point of view.

The fact that the Australians took three of our best wickets for nine runs and that our own bowlers got the visitors out twice for ridiculously small scores (even making allowance for the absence of Bradman and Fingleton) surely shows that there was nothing 'impossible' about the wicket.

If Australia had gone in and made 1,000 in reply to our 903 something might have been said for the suggestion, and it is a great pity that they were not afforded the opportunity of trying with their full strength to see if they could do so.

As things turned out there seems to be no reason for supposing that they would not have been fairly and squarely beaten in any event. Why 'crab' our victory?

Sigma
London NW8

SIR – In cricket could not the teams bat and field alternately from each interval? This would give the public an opportunity of seeing the play of each side in one day; would give equal conditions of the wicket; batsmen and bowlers would not have to endure excessive strain; and closer competition would be possible.

The toss of the coin would not then decide the match, neither would the weather influence it to the same extent, and the players' work would be 'spread over' and opportunities equalised.

Hugh Cornwall
London SE27

SIR – All praise to Mr Howard Marshall for his frank comments. The Oval game was the 20th Test against Australia I have witnessed. It is the one I want most to forget. It is a travesty of the game of cricket to see a batsman like Hardstaff adding 73 to his score in two and a quarter hours with 700 on the board. If this is what playing to a finish means, some of us will cry, 'Give us the draws of yesterday'. The unfinished match at Lord's was far more interesting.

As to Hutton, those who, like myself, saw Bradman's 334 will modify our transports. A difference of 30 runs is nothing to the fact that Bradman scored his runs in half the time on a Leeds wicket and did not slow up when approaching R.E. Foster's figure of 287. Of Hassett's innings it has been said that it was 'worthy of a proper cricket match'. It is sad that an Australian should have to be singled out for such praise.

W. Kent
London SW4

31 AUGUST 1938

SIR – A groundsman was reported in the papers some time ago to have stated, with regard to the Test pitch he had prepared, that it was good for a fortnight. No pitch should be good for a fortnight, and it is high time the authorities insisted upon a return to normal wickets. Only in that way will batsman and bowler meet again on level terms and scores return to less astronomical dimensions.

There seems to be no real reason why present arrangements as to time and toss should be altered, but over-preparation of wickets should be stopped. A score of 200 by a first-class batsman is not hailed now as an outstanding performance. It should be – and would be – if bowlers were able to obtain more assistance from the pitch. Let us in future have Tests fought out on pitches which have not been doctored and which have not been kept inviolate for four years.

R. Kendall
Hove

SIR – Might I suggest that the 'perfect' pitch should be preserved so that there may be fewer injuries, but that the ball, instead of being smooth leather which gets slippery with perspiration and has only a seam to help the fingers, should have a pimpled surface like that of a golf ball.

This, with the seam added, would give the bowler a chance to grip better and impart spin. The ball would also grip better on the ground for purposes of break. It should not be beyond the power of golf-ball manufacturers to produce quickly such a ball of the same size and weight as the leather one.

M.H. Bush
Hale

2 SEPTEMBER 1938

SIR – Sir Charles Hyde compares 'timeless' Test cricket with a chess match by mail. It is only fair to the game of chess, commonly looked upon as the slowest of games, to point out that in all international and other chess tournaments there is a strict time limit for moves.

Lincoln Chandler
Kingston-on-Thames

SIR – There is uncertainty in the public mind as to the meaning of 'doped' wickets, and the method and material employed. As honorary secretary of one of our county cricket clubs I can speak with some knowledge.

One method is partly to fill a tank with water. Into this some cow dung is placed and vigorously stirred. The mixture is evenly distributed over the pitch by a garden watering can.

The effects are 1) that the pace of the wicket is modified by the elastic layer, and 2) the wicket is made non-responsive to spin bowling by reason of the greasy film on the surface.

O'Reilly, the Australian bowler, recently informed me that he has been quite unable on such 'doped' wickets to turn the ball in the slightest degree. This is the whole art and subtlety of spin bowling nullified. The method I have described is practically in general use.

Honorary Secretary

19 MAY 1945

BRIGHTER CRICKET

SIR – From long experience, supported by a recent analytical study of *Wisden,* I am convinced that the chief bugbear to brighter cricket is that often debatable, always unsatisfactory, stab-in-the-back mode of getting out – stumping.

The brake the fear of this inglorious exit imposes on a batsman's enterprise is beyond computation, yet the percentage of 'kills' stumping registers in a season is so small as to be out of proportion to the great harm it does in slowing up the game. Abolition of this constrictive rule would fully be compensated by the number of catches which would inevitably arise from the resultant brighter cricket, not to mention upon the certainty of many additional run-outs.

Ross Anson
Bournemouth

28 AUGUST 1945

BRIGHTENING CRICKET

SIR – In spite of the absence of many pre-War personalities, how much more interesting this year's Test matches have been as games than, say, those of 1934 and 1938.

This, I think, is because there have been none of those mammoth record-breaking scores which were becoming so monotonous.

People were growing tired of seeing, or reading about, the same few batsmen piling up runs relentlessly day after day.

If we could go back to the days when 300 was considered a good, and probably a winning, total for an innings there would be some hope that cricket will be able to hold its own as a summer sport with its many modern competitors.

T. Gascoigne
Keswick

15 JULY 1946

VARSITY VETERAN

SIR – I am afraid that in my report of the university match I credited the Mackinnon of Mackinnon with a single in excess of his proper score. He is 98, having been born on 9 April, 1848, a few months before W.G. Grace.

A ball, yellow with the years, was taken out of the relics case in the Long Room of the Pavilion for his inspection. It was the one with which F.C. Cobden did the hat-trick that enabled Cambridge to beat Oxford by two runs in 1870. The Mackinnon, who played for Cambridge, is the only survivor of that match.

E.W. Swanton
Lord's
London NW8

30 JULY 1946

THE HAMBLEDON MEN

SIR – Peterborough tells us of efforts to secure a copy of the historic Hambledon bat for the forthcoming Regency match at Brighton.

May I point out that if one of the teams is to represent the old Hambledon Club the members of it will not require top hats? The old Hambledon men wore a costume of their own design, consisting of velvet caps, knee breeches, stockings and buckle shoes. They travelled to their matches in a caravan.

Their opponents usually played in top hats and their ordinary clothes. Perhaps their sporting attire helped the Hambledon men to win so many of their matches!

My great-great-grandfather ('old Richard Nyren') led his men against All England in 31 matches, of which they won 25 and lost only six.

Richard P. Nyren
Caterham

5 AUGUST 1946
BRIGHTER CRICKET

SIR – Cricket is neither 'slow' nor 'old-fashioned', though it is often described as that by people who do not understand the spirit of the game. Nevertheless, wise and enterprising changes might enliven the sport and invite a wider public.

Firstly, I suggest that championship matches should be played on Sundays. Matches could run from Saturday to Monday and from Wednesday to Friday, the day off for players to fall on Thursdays. This would bring in a host of spectators and perhaps be the best answer to the clubs' financial problems.

Secondly, the teams in the county championship have not changed for years, and some have been consistent losers season after season. There is no penalty for being at the bottom of the table. Why not learn from the Association football system, and relegate the lowest teams to the minor counties? This would provide a stimulus to win matches, even among teams who could not hope to win the championship, and it would also give opportunities for minor counties to rise into the main championship sphere. If Leicestershire and Somerset and Glamorgan can compete, why not Cheshire or Devon or Durham?

Thirdly, I would suggest that the batsmen's average scoring speeds should be published. Then we shall know who are our best run-getters. The men with the fastest averages consistent with big scores would be heroes, and what batsman would want to be called the slowest?

Flight Officer E.L. Normanton, RAF
Orpington

22 AUGUST 1946
WAS IT CRICKET?

SIR – I have just read in *The Daily Telegraph* during the Test match, 'Compton kicked the ball into the stumps at the bowler's end, with Merchant out of his ground. No one could remember seeing a wicket fall in such a way before.'

My cricketing days date from those of S.M.J. Woods, Gregor McGregor, and G.J.V. Weigall at Cambridge University in 1887. In those times I cannot recollect that the foot was ever used to 'field the ball'.

This is a comparatively modern invention, and is developing very rapidly, I am sorry to see, in every kind of cricket.

It is well to remember that there is such a game as football, which, in my view, should not be confused with the grand old game of cricket.

J. Herbert Twamley
Bedford

23 AUGUST 1946
WAS IT CRICKET?

SIR – Denis Compton, in using his feet to 'field a ball', was not making use of a 'modern cricket invention', as one of your correspondents suggests. It has been recognised for years.

I saw W.G. Grace, in his last Gentlemen versus Players match, deliberately stamp his foot on a ball which was passing him, and only last week R.W.V. Robins, fielding against Kent at Lord's, received merited applause for a left-footed interception of a wide, fast-moving ball that was reminiscent of Eddie Hapgood or Jesse Pennington at their best.

After all, if a bowler can break through a batsman's defence and rap his pads, and the batting side gain by any ensuing leg-byes, surely a fieldsman can use his feet.

W.J. O'Reilly
London SW18

24 AUGUST 1946
WAS IT CRICKET?

SIR – Yes, in my view, it was. Merchant was run out under No. 28 of the Rules of Cricket and also under Rule 41, which reads, inter alia, 'The fieldsman may stop the ball with any part of his person.'

Major B.J.N. Titmas
South Woodford

15 JULY 1948
GRACE'S FIELDING

SIR – In Mr Campbell Dixon's article on W.G. Grace, the centenary of whose birth occurs next Sunday, no mention is made of his marvellous fielding. One example of this I had the delight to witness myself.

In a Test match at Lord's in the Eighties 'W.G.' was at point. Trott cut the first ball of the match very hard only about a foot from the ground straight to him. The G.O.M. was down like a flash, in spite of his girth, and caught it between his feet.

I think that is a correct description, if my memory after all these years serves me aright, of the most sensational incident in Test match history.

Hugh B. Fitch
London WC2

SIR – Mr Campbell Dixon's article revived memories of Lord's and 'W.G.' with whom I spent a day over 40 years ago 'beagling' in Surrey. He took charge of me and showed me the short cuts. We finished up at a pub, drank beer, smoked clay pipes, sang songs and told tales.

Over 80 years ago, my father had a business in St John's Wood, and while tending his sheep in Lord's cricket ground he used to watch the members of MCC play cricket in top-hats. There was no gate in those days.

C.R.H. Randall
Stourport-on-Severn

17 JULY 1948

GRACE'S TWOPENCE

SIR – In the old days many boys living near the Oval somehow got on to the ground after school.

One evening five or six of us were bowling to W.G. Grace and I bowled him out. In the pavilion afterwards he gave me twopence – a lot of money to a boy then.

E.T. Cass
Halesworth

SIR – Mr Campbell Dixon's article on W.G. Grace, the centenary of whose birth occurs this weekend, reminds me of a happy incident.

When a little girl, living near Scarborough, I was a real cricket enthusiast both as spectator and player. During the annual festival I was sitting in the pavilion, proudly holding my new spliced bat.

Grace noticed me as he was going down the steps, and he asked if he could try it. So together we went on to the field, where I bowled to his batting.

Needless to say, a crowd gathered round us, much amused by the big man with the small bat.

Mabel Tansley
London SW3

30 JULY 1948

PLAYING THE GAME

SIR – In Mr E.W. Swanton's excellent commentaries on the Test at Leeds he suggested that the English captain made use of the heavy motor roller with the intention of affecting the pitch adversely, legalising this action by using the pitch for his own batsmen for two overs.

These are clever tactics, and a good healthy crack, if it could have been produced, would have served us happily. Yet one would express the hope that the Old Country might set an example rather than follow a bad one in how to play the game.

Reverend H.A.H. Lea
Edgware

1 JULY 1950

RUNNERS-OUT

SIR – Why is no official recognition given to a player for a 'run-out'?

Fielding is not the least important part of cricket, and its improvement is worthy of every effort of encouragement. In the case of a batsman caught out, the name of the fielder making the catch is recorded, and even when a man is stumped, so is the name of the stumper.

Could not, then, the rules be altered to enable the successful 'runner-out's' name to be given in the official records? When the wicket is actually thrown down by the wicketkeeper, his name could also be given as, for instance, 'run out Yardley (Evans)'.

S. Darrington
Banstead

1 AUGUST 1950

CRICKET TEA TIME

SIR – The tea interval was a charming social interlude in country-house and village cricket. How did it infiltrate into county cricket? Possibly at the instigation of the catering industry?

I do not know when it occurred, but I think it is not in the interests of first-class cricket. In a three-day match nearly an hour is lost. A batsman has to play himself in again, a bowler to find his length.

My cricket memories go back more than 50 years. 'W.G.' and the heroes of the cricket world played as hard and keenly in the Seventies and Eighties as those of today. True, the spin bowler was not so much in evidence, but they played on natural wickets and the fear of a 'shooter' was always before them. Surely men in full strength and vigour could do without sustenance from 2 to 6.30 p.m.

E.A. Pole
Leeds

4 AUGUST 1950
CRICKET TEA TIME

SIR – Mr E.A. Pole suggests the tea interval infiltrated into county cricket from village or country-house cricket. It may be so, but where did it start?

I was playing village and club cricket for many years up to 1900 in East Sussex. Neither in village cricket or even in our club cricket week was a tea interval ever known. Play began at 2 or 2.30 p.m. and ended at 6.30 p.m.

In village cricket it was no uncommon thing for each side to complete two innings. In club cricket this was unusual, but play did not cease till the time for drawing stumps, and no one left the ground except perhaps to get a glass of beer at the nearest public house.

When I moved to Devonshire I found the tea interval was sometimes but not always taken in village matches. Personally, I always felt it spoilt the game.

John D.H. Patch
Newton Abbot

7 AUGUST 1950
CRICKET TEA TIME

SIR – Play in a normal day's first-class cricket match extends from 11.30 a.m. until 6.30 p.m., including 40 minutes for lunch and 20 minutes for tea. This allows for six hours of actual play, and that is surely an adequate ration for cricketers called upon to play for six days in nearly every week of the summer.

If, as Mr E.A. Pole suggests, the tea interval were abolished, teams would frequently find themselves in the field for some four and a half hours without a break, and their physical condition at the end of play is easy to imagine.

Conditions in the Seventies and Eighties were very different from those today. At no time during that period did more than nine counties compete for the championship. That meant that the average cricketer played in only half as many matches during the summer as his present-day counterpart. Hence the need for the respite afforded by a tea interval did not exist.

David Moore
Bristol

11 AUGUST 1950

HARVEST CRICKETERS

SIR – Some years ago I had an experience which puts the cricketers' tea interval in another light.

We were playing against a village side and our opponents batted first. This was followed by tea in the pavilion, provided by the squire.

When the home side took the field I missed several players who had attracted my attention before tea and then found that the fielding side was completely new. This was an arrangement made to suit the harvest. It was so established that it was not thought necessary even to mention it to the visiting captain.

I have little doubt that three XIs enjoyed the lavish spread.

R.J. Mowll
Haywards Heath

14 AUGUST 1950
CRICKETERS' HOURS

SIR – Mr David Moore's letter seems to suggest that modern first-class cricketers will collapse if deprived of their tea interval.

Nowadays there is a tendency, not confined to your correspondent, to imply that they are under strain, both physically and mentally. This seems to me not only to be a disservice to a great game, but to be at variance with the facts.

The game (or work, if preferred) is played in the open air and under healthy conditions. The period of play (or work) is theoretically six days per week, but owing to rain or the early termination of matches, it is, in practice, often less. The hours of play, again, are theoretically only six per day, but in practice often less. Moreover, approximately half the period is spent, not in the field, but in the pavilion resting.

It is true there is much tiring travelling between matches. Some players, too, go overseas with touring teams in the winter, but they are only a handful of the large number of county players, and even they have a long break and a sea voyage in which to recuperate between seasons.

L.S. Emms
Dorking

22 AUGUST 1950
FIELDERS' STANCE

SIR – I think the view expounded by Lieutenant-Colonel C.C. Eccles on the way to stand while fielding near the wicket was completely disregarded by the West Indies in the Test match at the Oval.

I particularly noticed the short leg fielders. At the beginning of the delivery of each ball, the three or four short legs started to crouch with their legs wide apart and simultaneously each pulled up his trousers; the drill equalled anything on the barrack square.

V.J. Roynon
Oxford

5 AUGUST 1953
RUN-GETTING ORGIES

SIR – I cannot agree with your correspondents that it has been a disappointing tale of four doleful Test matches. In each of them the play has been of absorbing interest.

Orgies of run-getting and huge totals can be merely boring. It is when a real fight develops that the greatest of games is seen at its best, irrespective of the talent of the teams engaged. Why the agitation for a definite result at the Oval?

The first four matches have shown that there is little between the sides and honours even at the end of the series would not seem unjust.

Captain G.C. Fryer, R.N. (Retired)
Saxmundham

6 AUGUST 1953
DEFENSIVE CRICKET

SIR – Mr A.L. Gillibrand says: 'You can only bat as well as the bowler will let you.' I would remind him that Compton in his heyday, and many other solid batsmen, held precisely the opposite view. It is that a bowler bowls as well as the batsman will allow him.

Gerald R. Smith
Chester

7 AUGUST 1953

PARTISAN CRICKET

SIR – Some of your correspondents fail to take into account that, for the vast majority of us, it is essential to be thoroughly partisan to enjoy a game.

If the spectator is sufficiently keen for one side to win or, failing that, not be beaten, then any sort of defensive or negative tactics seem justified and can be absurdly interesting. But to enjoy a match the result of which holds no particular interest bright cricket is necessary.

The English batting in the last Test was to me interesting and even breathtaking at times. But only because I am an Englishman. I would not pretend it was really cricket in any sense of the word.

K.G. Green
Bramhall

8 AUGUST 1953

AGGRESSIVE CRICKET

SIR – May I partner Mr Gerald R. Smith in attacking the bowling of Mr A.L. Gillibrand? To say that 'you can bat only as well as the bowler lets you' is to admit that the bowler is your master. One of England's best bowlers said of W.G. Grace: 'I put the ball where I wants, but the doctor, he puts it where he wants.'

Beauty is as beauty does, and if the many 'beautiful' batsmen who have recently played for England cannot make runs, let them be supplanted by those who can, even if it is by methods of ugly and brutal aggression. Those whose aesthetic susceptibilities would be offended can always seek solace at the ballet.

From among our competent batsmen let us choose for

England those who have the will to murder the bowling – and any fieldsmen impertinent enough to dare to stand too close.

Lieutenant-Colonel R.E. Collins
Andover

11 AUGUST 1953
From Sir Home Gordon

SIR – It may be of interest to recall what Ranjitsinhji said to me both in England and when I was his guest in India for the Durbar.

'In first-class cricket,' he declared, 'the standard of batting always is only just superior to that of contemporaneous bowling.'

Home Gordon
Rottingdean

13 AUGUST 1953
BOWLER VERSUS BATSMAN

SIR – The letter from Sir Home Gordon quoting Prince Ranjitsinhji leaves out of account that from, say, 1860 to 1890 the bowler was on top of the batsman, not vice versa.

The Prince also said, and I repeated in print, that in cricket everything that matters is elementary.

The Prince was the acutest judge of our difficult beautiful summer game which, by the way, is not as good a game as polo.

C.B. Fry
London SW1

15 AUGUST 1953

IT'S NOT CRICKET, SIR!
From Canon D.H.S. Mould

SIR – A match like that at Lord's should not be advertised as 'cricket'. The man who pays good money to see cricket, and is served up with something else has a fair grievance. At least he should be warned before he enters the ground what he will see.

I suggest that before a match the captains should decide what game they are going to play, and that their decision should be posted up in big letters outside the ground. If they post up 'cricket', let them play cricket as the plain man understands it; if they decide simply to try not to get out in three days, let them advertise 'blockit'. Then the spectator will be warned and nobody will have been deceived.

D.H.S. Mould
Newcastle-on-Tyne

SIR – One's reaction to Mr E.W. Swanton's rightly indignant report on the Middlesex versus Surrey match fiasco is that the presumably able-bodied teams are so mentally and physically tired that they are unable to play cricket in the right spirit.

Perhaps they might be better employed helping with the harvest or something similarly useful.

Randle Jackson
Lord's Cricket Ground
London NW8

21 AUGUST 1953

SIR – England has recovered the Ashes and all's well that ends well – for England. But can any game beat a Test match as a sheer gamble?

For four days the teams at the Oval were able to play unin-
terruptedly. Perhaps the better side won. But if before play
began on the fourth day there had been a downpour, which in
this country would have been nothing unusual, England's
wickets might well have fallen like ninepins, we might easily
have lost the match, and the rubber would have gone again to
Australia. And if, marred by persistent rain, the match had run
its full course of six days and then ended inconclusively, the
Ashes would still have remained with Australia.

Surely these Test teams cross the seas to prove in hard
combat who is the abler – and not to take part in a gamble. But
the plain fact is that Test match results are primarily determined by the fluke of the weather at any given time, and incidentally by the spin of the coin.

L.J. Reedman
Birmingham

22 AUGUST 1953
CRICKET AT ITS BEST

SIR – Before the memories of a great Test match recede into
history, may I pay tribute to two features in it which seem to
me to have a special message for the countless young cricketers who no doubt followed it with breathless interest?

The first was the brilliance, hostility and courage of the
Australian fielding, sustained long after any real hope can have
survived, and indeed until the last ball of the match. Surely this
should be an inspiration and a challenge to every boy, for in no
department of the game is practice and determination more
certain to yield its reward.

The second was the spirit in which the whole game was
fought by both sides, intensely combative, always friendly.
Here, too, was a lesson for all our young cricketers. For there
is only one way in which to play cricket, whether in the middle

or in practice, and that is as hard as they can, and the harder they play it the more enjoyable they will find it. That is, of course, provided always they remember that they are playing not only against but with their opponents, and that there is a price beyond which victory should never be bought.

When Mr Hassett and his team sail for home, they will be leaving the Ashes behind, but they should be taking with them the gratitude of all who care about the future of English cricket for all they have done to show the next generation how the game should always be played.

H.S. Altham
Chairman
MCC Youth Cricket Association
London NW1

25 AUGUST 1953

SIR – We have become so used to having our national failures explained, in the cricketing world as elsewhere, as the result of post-War depression, protein starvation, lack of initiative, poor leadership and super-tax, that we seem to have grown thoroughly defeatist.

Now England have won the Ashes – on a good wicket, against the toss, and by dint of thoroughly good batting and bowling against the best Australia could produce.

The professional pessimists have shown themselves very good at explaining our failures. To what do they attribute our success?

R. Corrin Bell
Bury

29 DECEMBER 1954
INTIMIDATORY

SIR – Some 20 years ago the use by a bowler of alleged intimida-
tory tactics nearly provoked a Commonwealth crisis. Today this
same bowling is looked upon as part of the stock-in-trade of every
fast bowler. That does not alter the fact that deliberately intimi-
dating tactics are not, never have been, and never will be cricket.

The chief objection is that the ball is not designed to take a
wicket, but simply to soften up the batsman by a process of
frightening and unnerving him, or even possibly injuring him
before a ball is bowled. Thus it is designed to take advantage
of his state of nerves to get him out. It would be just as logical
for the bowler to drug his opponent's luncheon coffee, or spray
him between overs with tear-gas, and much less trouble to
both.

Are we to wait for the inevitable fatality before steps are
taken to exorcise cricket's evil demon? It could quite simply be
exorcised by a definition bringing the 'bumper' into the category of 'No-balls'.

R.M.G. Lloyd
London N8

7 JANUARY 1955
WICKET OR PITCH?

SIR – I see reference in both your leading article and Mr E.W.
Swanton's reports on the third Test match to the Melbourne
'wicket'.

Cannot it be established that the stretch of turf, which is
horizontal and measures 22 yards, is in fact the pitch? The
wicket, on the other hand, is that wooden contrivance of
three stumps and two bails which form Tyson's target: only
the bails being in the horizontal plane, and the stumps

remaining upright according to the skill or otherwise of the batsman.

If the pitch is to be called a wicket, then at the opening of the game the wickets, one assumes, will have to be 'wicketed' instead of pitched.

Oliver Sandbach
Twickenham

13 JANUARY 1955
AT THE WICKET

SIR – Mr Oliver Sandbach states that the stretch of turf which is horizontal and measures 22 yards is in fact the pitch, while the wicket is the wooden contrivance of three stumps and two bails.

But I am sure he is wrong to condemn Mr E.W. Swanton for referring to the 22-yard pitch as the wicket. It has always been so called.

Even before the 1914–18 War Lord Hawke stated in his 'Glossary of Cricket Terms': 'The wicket is the parallelogram formed by imaginary lines drawn from the off-stump at one end to the leg-stump at the other, and from the leg-stump at one end to the off-stump at the other. Also, the three stumps with two bails on them are called the wicket.'

The pitch is the whole area of the ground that has been mown and rolled, and on which the wickets have been erected. The pitch of the ball is the spot where the ball propelled by the bowler touches the earth.

Rupert Pennick
Stansted Mountfitchet
Essex

28 JANUARY 1955

STUMPED

SIR – Mr H.H. Thomas might have ended his letter with the cricket conundrum to beat them all: Why it is that wickets are pitched to start the day's play but stumps are drawn to end it?

F.A. Allcott
London W1

SIR – How does a batsman become 'leg-before-wicket' to the whole of the playing surface between the six stumps if this area be, as some correspondents assert, 'the wicket'?

H. Barrington Brown
Warminster
Wiltshire

29 JANUARY 1955

WICKETS OR STUMPS

SIR – Mr H.H. Thomas seems unable to differentiate between the words 'stump' and 'wicket'. The *Oxford Dictionary* clearly states that a wicket comprises one set of three stumps and two bails.

In the light of this etymology, it is not difficult to understand why a batsman may lose his leg, middle or off stump, but not his leg, middle or off wicket. Similarly, a bowler bowls round or over a wicket because three stumps equal one wicket. Again, 'stumps are drawn' because each stump is plucked out of the ground individually; if three stumps were drawn intact with the bails simultaneously the wicket would be drawn.

G. Bernard Edgeler
London SE25

1 FEBRUARY 1955
'HOW'S THAT?'

SIR – Is the ball at mid-wicket when it disarranges the middle stump, and is the wicket-keeper the person who tends the sacred turf?

David J. Birkett
Gravesend

SIR – I agree that 'batting on a sticky pitch' is an unlikely term but, used in cricket match description, it is technically correct.

Before the commencement of a match wickets are pitched, and the site chosen, therefore, can rightly be termed the 'pitch'. In a similar manner the part of a street selected by a street vendor is known as his pitch.

In cricketing language the areas referred to as the 'wicket' and the 'pitch' are obviously synonymous.

W.E. Dowdall
Ruislip

8 JANUARY 1955
POETIC CRICKET

SIR – Frank Tyson's seven for 27 in the third Test match, a feat achieved in spite of, or because of, his alleged engaging habit of quoting Wordsworth to himself in the course of his 18-yard run up to the wicket, gives rise to some speculations.

Is he alone in this quaint and surely unusual practice? Did Compton, caught off his glove in a presumed effort to steer the ball through the slips, whisper to himself: 'This was the most unkindest cut of all'?

Did May, in dealing with the bowling on its merits in his second innings of 91, recall his Omar.

'The ball no question makes of Ayes or Noes.
But right or left, as strikes the player goes'?

Did Bailey, while holding the fort with ten runs in an hour, echo to himself: *'J'y suis, j'y reste'*? It seems hardly likely that Evans after his brilliant display will have had any notions of emulating the Ancient Mariner who 'stoppeth one in three'. But perhaps Statham, surveying the outstretched hands of his behind-the-wicket fielders, said to himself: 'I see you stand like greyhounds in the slips.'

And, finally, did Bedser, whose omission from the last two Test matches recalls a famous cartoon of many years ago enti-tled 'Dropping the Pilot', murmur to himself: 'Farewell, a long farewell, to all my greatness'?

No doubt, Sir, your more erudite contributors will enjoy themselves immeasurably in enlarging the field of quotation.

A.W. Black
Eastbourne

25 JANUARY 1955

BOWLING THE GOOGLY

SIR – In his letter on old-time cricketers Mr Hedley Ashley-Cooper seems rather scathing. I would like to know why he 'debunks' my late brother as the author of the 'googly'. I can assure him Jack Hearne did not share his views.

I would suggest he consults Sir Pelham Warner or L. Braund, survivors of the 1904 team who won the Ashes. The Austral-ians, who were victims of the 'googly', called these novelties (to them) 'Bosies' and continued to do so in 1915 (possibly they still do) when McCarthy gave me his opinion.

The original 'googly' was a ball which broke either way, or not at all, with the same action. Incidentally, this method of bowling was the ultimate development of flicking a tennis ball across the slates of a billiard table under repair.

N. Bosanquet
Oxford

30 JULY 1956
TEST WICKETS

SIR – As an old cricketer, I find it very irritating to read all this nonsense about the Test wickets at Manchester and at Leeds. Are we to make our Test wickets to suit the likes and dislikes of the visiting sides or should they take things as they come, just as our fellows have to do when they go overseas?

I remember that when Australia had Gregory and Macdonald, the wickets Down Under were as hard and as fast as human ingenuity could make them. But when they relied almost exclusively on Grimmett and O'Reilly, those wickets were of a totally different character.

England then had no complaint and did not make one. Nor did the Australian press on England's behalf.

Would anyone like to tell me what happened, or could have happened, to the Manchester wicket during lunch interval on Friday to account for the difference between the play before and after lunch?

For that day's cricket, only one of two explanations is possible. Either the England spinners, Lock and Laker, are a lot better than their opposite numbers, Ian Johnson and Benaud, or the last seven England batsmen are better than all the Australian batsmen put together. Take your choice.

Percy G.H. Fender
London W1

1 AUGUST 1956

SIR – Mr Percy Fender's letter respecting the current Test match was timely and apt.

From some of the comments about the Old Trafford pitch, one might almost think that, after their 'tail' had made such a vigorous showing, the England team brought some mysterious force to bear so that it was impossible for the Australians to do anything with the bat.

What a pity it is that our friends from Down Under give such a bad impression of themselves when things go wrong for them. One is forced to the conclusion that, whereas cricket for us remains a game, for the Australians it has become largely a business, in which sportsmanship plays a relatively minor part.

S. Langford
London SW1

7 AUGUST 1956

SIR – Mr E.W. Swanton, giving the Test match position in review, fails to make one thing clear. How did the groundsman who prepared a wicket which would be excellent for the first two days and thereafter crumble, know that the English would win the toss? And what would have been said had the Australians gone in first and made a fine first-innings total?

There seem to be some Englishmen who revel in the view that the English cannot possibly win by fair means, and therefore must have used foul.

M. Lavars Harry
Ashtead
Surrey

11 SEPTEMBER 1956
C.B. FRY

SIR – Your obituary of the admirable C.B. Fry has well shown his pre-eminence as an athlete, footballer and cricketer, but let us not forget that he was also a keen rider to hounds.

He said: 'No sport that does not involve the companionship of a horse can be as good as one that does.'

George Forster-Knight
Market Drayton

14 SEPTEMBER 1956
FRY IN THE SADDLE

SIR – C.B. Fry was much more than a keen rider to hounds, as Mr Forster-Knight submits. I recall even now the thrill that some of us had on seeing him at a Pytchley meet sitting his horse as horsemanship was then understood and later finding that he was thoroughly enjoying himself alongside those nearest to hounds.

He was as perturbed about the acrobatics that are hailed as horsemanship as he was about the rabbit-like effeteness that is now endured as batsmanship. 'I must admit,' he wrote to me only recently, 'that if batting goes on like this, cricket will earn complete disrepute, quite ordinary bowlers bowling quite ordinary stuff, and batsmen treating it as though it were a bag of cobras. On Saturday I saw two strokes all day.'

If he had had his £10,000 a year he would have been an outstanding M.F.H. and he would also probably have played polo for England, as he always considered polo the best of all the ball games.

George Drummond
Mount Rule

SIR – Shortly after the First World War I met C.B. Fry at the winter sports at Wengen. After a few days' practice on the ice rink as a complete novice, he was attracted by my wife's figure skating and waltzing, and asked her to teach him to waltz.

With some trepidation she did so, and although considerably shorter and less robust than he was, she managed to support him and pull him through the intricacies of edges and turns.

It was an interesting and at times awesome sight, and compelled other skaters to keep a respectable distance from uncontrollable flying legs and skates.

Anyhow his keenness was not to be denied, and although C.B. would never have become a 'ballet dancer' on ice, he eventually acquired a certain proficiency which made his waltzing less dangerous.

E.M. Gollance
London N5

20 JUNE 1958

A HIT FOR 47

SIR – Some time in the 1870s my uncle by marriage, Colonel (then Captain) Renny Tallyeur, a famous athlete and one of the hardest-hitting bats of his time, hit a 13, without overthrow, on the R.E. ground on Chatham Lines, then innocent of boundaries.

Some time in the late 1890s I can testify to having seen one Russell, who I believe kept wicket for Essex, hit a six, without overthrow, from an off-drive at Lord's that just failed to reach the boundary.

About the same period I saw a ball hit for 47. It was at a scratch game of a few boys on our lawn at Norton Lodge, Freshwater.

The ball was hit into a tree, and the striker, being the biggest boy present, carried the ruling that it could not be lost so long as it could be seen. Accordingly the batsmen continued to run until a bamboo pole could be procured from the house to dislodge it.

Esme Wingfield-Stratford
Berkhamsted

2 DECEMBER 1958
MAY VERSUS AUSTRALIA

SIR – How often in a first-class cricket match has a batsman of one team not only scored a century in each innings but also, in each innings, scored more runs himself than the total scored in each innings by the opposing team?

I refer, of course, to the recent match in Australia, MCC versus An Australian XI, when Peter May himself scored 140 and 114 for the MCC and An Australian XI 128 and 103.

John S. Dodd
Eastbourne

11 DECEMBER 1958
CRICKET TRAVESTY

SIR – I was glad to see Mr E.W. Swanton's disapproving remarks about the slowness of the run-getting in the Test match, and in such matches generally, though a rate of about 130 a day would seem to deserve more than the mild censure he gives it.

Mr Swanton says it is not easy to see how the present stranglehold of the bowlers is to be relaxed. May I say that the solution is very simple really?

The trouble about Test matches is that they are not so much a game these days as an international crisis, if one is to judge by the more sensational newspapers. If we could go back to the fact that these men are playing a game there would not be the same tension, the same necessity to bore everyone by making certain of not losing, regardless of whether by doing so one makes it impossible to win.

If somebody sold the Ashes and used the money to give all concerned a drink or two, they might go on to the field with the idea of enjoying themselves, and would then have some chance of giving enjoyment to those who pay to watch them. If that is too fanciful, would it yet be possible to get into the heads of the players and of a great many reporters also, that it does not matter whether we lose the Ashes or not? What does matter is that a good game should not be insulted by a travesty of playing it.

T.D.S. Broadbent
Temple Grafton

12 DECEMBER 1958
CRICKET TRAVESTY

SIR – Much scratching of eminent heads and pens results in occasional amendments to the laws of cricket in a desperate attempt to brighten the game. Judging by the affair at Brisbane, the scratching has not gone deep enough.

In my humble opinion the remedy lies in the hands of the cricket correspondents. I am sure we should see no repetition of the Brisbane business if in the columns of the newspapers the next day the whole affair had been relegated to a few lines at the bottom of a column, which could well have read:

'On the fourth day of the first Test match at Brisbane the MCC scored 106 runs in five hours against quite good bowling and on a good wicket. In his waking moments your correspondent saw nothing worthy of reporting.'

R.P. Raikes
Pleshey

13 DECEMBER 1958

REFLECTIONS ON THE BRISBANE DISPLAY

SIR – Congratulations to my friend Mr E.W. Swanton on his brilliant and sensible comments from Brisbane.

'A bowler,' he reminds us, 'will only bowl as well as he is allowed to.' As one who once was himself a professional off-spinner (better than Burke!), may I heartily say, 'How right you are, Swanton!'

Various apologetic experts on the spot have assured us that it is unreasonable to expect our modern scientific batsmen to make strokes if:

a) the bowling is accurate;
b) the bowling is inaccurate;
c) there is too much grass on the wicket;
d) there is not too much grass on the wicket;
e) the field is set 'tight';
f) the field is spread out.

How do our contemporary heroes of the willow expect to receive the ball – on a plate with parsley?

Neville Cardus
London W1

SIR – It is perhaps opportune to assess the influence of that great cricketer, Sir Leonard Hutton, on English Test cricket. He was one of the greatest batsmen we have seen, but I suggest that he is more responsible than any other living cricketer for the malaise into which Test match cricket has fallen.

He is a Yorkshireman who earned his living as a cricketer. Cricket to him was a business, and he brought all the admirable qualities of the Yorkshireman to making his business succeed. And the successful businessman plays safe.

Sir Leonard played safe. As captain of one side of participants in a Test match his primary object seems always to have been to avoid losing it.

But what so many of us cannot understand is why Sir Leonard's successor, who has not reached the top the hard way, should apparently approach a Test match in the same frame of mind, and allow his team to do likewise.

After all, does it matter very much whether we beat Australia or not? Is it not infinitely more important that the matches should be played in such a spirit that both players and spectators enjoy them? And anyhow, if cricket has become purely a business, surely the MCC should be wondering how soon they will have to shut the shop for lack of customers.

J.W. Kernick
Chiddingfold

17 DECEMBER 1958
TEST BATTING

SIR – If Mr Peter May is going to experiment with the batting after the Brisbane Test, may I suggest that the Ingleby-Mackenzie Hampshire experiment be tried? This experiment merely consists of regarding the bat as an instrument of offence, and results in quick runs, cricket enjoyed by players and spectators, packed stands, and a game quite unlike the one endured by the post-War spectator.

Is it not time that the press, the county captains and county committees indulged in some plain speaking to those players whose aim appears to be the extinction of cricket?

J.E. Butcher
Maresfield

7 JANUARY 1959

UMPIRE IS HANDICAPPED
From Brigadier Sir John Smyth, V.C., M.P.

SIR – I was much impressed with the first few words of the commentary from Melbourne by your excellent cricket commentator, Mr E.W. Swanton, describing the death-rattle of British hopes in the second Test match. He was commenting on the growing criticism of the legality of the Australian I. Meckiff's bowling action.

We never like to squeal when we are getting beaten, and we are certainly not doing so now. Nevertheless, this is a matter which must inevitably arouse bad feelings and may spoil the remaining Tests and do the game of cricket no good.

Now who are the people who should settle the knotty problem as to whether Meckiff – quite unintentionally, I am sure – throws his faster ball? The Australian cricket controllers say that it is entirely a matter for the umpires. But is it?

If Meckiff threw every ball, as some people say another Australian bowler does, it might be possible for the umpire at the bowling end to make a decision. But the critics say that his action is open to suspicion only when he bowls his super-fast swerving kicker – the ball that gets the wickets. And a fast bowler who can claim Peter May's wicket three times within a few weeks in international cricket must have something.

No, the umpire at the bowler's end – and I am speaking of *fast* bowling – glues his eyes on the bowler's feet to see if he no-balls. It is difficult enough for him in all conscience to make that decision correctly and raise his eyes in a split second for a possible lbw or caught-at-the-wicket decision. He cannot possibly be watching the bowler's arm at the same time or he would require another eye in the top of his head.

This is a matter which must be decided by the players as a whole on the field and by the great ex-players of the game who are watching in the pavilion.

I quite realise that the controversy over Meckiff's bowling presents a difficult problem to the Australians. What is done cannot be undone. And I sympathise with them in their problem – which must be theirs alone as far as the present Tests are concerned. And I may say that I have a son who has settled in Australia, married there and had a family; so I am very pro-Australian.

But I do hope the critics will not continue to jump quite so heavily on Peter May – one of the grandest young athletes and sportsmen Britain has ever produced – just because things are not going his way at the moment. We have not lost the Ashes yet – and, even if we do, it will be nice to win them back in England next time.

J.G. Smyth
House of Commons

9 JANUARY 1959

THROWING

SIR – Few lovers of cricket will disagree with the excellent letter from Brigadier Sir John Smyth, V.C., M.P., on throwing. There is one point, however, which he does not cover.

Sir John mentions, quite understandably, the extreme difficulty of the umpire at the bowler's end, but says nothing about the square-leg umpire. Rule 26 of the Laws of Cricket is quite definite on the subject: '. . . if *either* umpire be not entirely satisfied of the absolute fairness of a delivery in this respect, he shall call, and signal "No-Ball" instantly upon delivery . . .'

Further, in view of the splendid TV pictures of the Test matches we are seeing on our screens, surely a good telescopic slow-motion film could settle the question once and for all, and before the matter assumes international complications.

Frederick W. Gant
Beeston

25 JUNE 1960

CRICKET PRECEDENTS

SIR – The no-balling of Griffin at Lord's must, surely, bring matters to a head. For my part, I have to admit that I could see (from a distance) very little, if any, difference between the deliveries which were no-balled and those which were not.

That, however, is beside the point, except for the fact that it must (with bowlers like Griffin, and different from some others) be a matter of extraordinary difficulty to decide what is and what is not a throw.

Let us think back in cricket history and remember that when the game was first played the bowler bowled *under-arm.* After some years, someone began to deliver the ball *round-arm*, and, after a few years of protest against this method (much like that which has now arisen over throwing) the round-arm method was legalised.

A few years later, someone began to bowl *over-arm,* and this also led to similar protests, but, again after a while, this over-arm method, too, was legalised.

The *real* unfairness about throwing is when one side does it and the other side is not allowed to do it.

There will always be differences of opinion as to whether any particular bowler throws or not, and such opinions may well be coloured by the locality in which the game is being played.

It might seem that the only way in which an 'international situation' can be avoided in future (perhaps next summer) would be doing what has been done before about, first, round-arm bowling and, later, over-arm bowling.

Percy G.H. Fender
London W1

28 JUNE 1960

THROWING

SIR – One hesitates before taking issue with so distinguished an authority and ex-player as Mr Percy G.H. Fender. But for my part I should be shocked and disappointed to see the problem of throwing solved in the way he suggests – by making a throw legal.

The present bowling action, than which there is nothing more exhilarating to watch, has evolved, as Mr Fender points out, in a natural sequence, from under-arm by way of round-arm to over-arm, by the successive legalisation of unorthodox actions.

Now I maintain that the throw has no place in this sequence, as Mr Fender would have us believe. In all previous bowling actions the final swing has been smooth and the bowler's arm has remained reasonably straight throughout, but in the throw there is a hideous jerk of the elbow at the moment of delivery.

Again, surely, the real unfairness of throwing is the advantage it gives the thrower in being able to produce a devastatingly fast and dangerous ball with extremely little prior warning to the batsman.

But to my mind the most powerful argument against throwing, and the reason why we must all hope that it will be speedily driven out of cricket, is that it threatens to destroy one of the most thrilling and beautiful aspects of the game – the glorious sight of a Lindwall or a Trueman accelerating up to the wicket and bowling.

N.A.J. Swanson
Peaslake

29 JUNE 1960

THROWING

SIR – I would let Griffin throw. Most cricketers would not throw any better than they can bowl. This would get away from all the trouble as to whether a cricketer throws or bowls.

Major R.G. Johnstone
Naval & Military Club
London W1

30 JUNE 1960
'DOGBERRYS OF CRICKET'

SIR – To compensate a crowd deprived of its money's worth after a premature ending of a Test match, an 'exhibition' game is played at Lord's.

Customary 'law' and 'rules' are put into abeyance in the name of public entertainment. For example, a team's innings is limited to 20 overs, and each player except one stumper is obliged to bowl two, and no more, overs.

In the free-and-easy atmosphere umpire Buller no-balls Griffin, already a marked and harassed young man, because of his suspect arm in seriously played and thoroughly 'legal' Test cricket. And Buller, together with some equally pompous supporters in the press box, justifies this solemn and severe consistency in light-hearted circumstances by telling us that he was umpiring in a game of cricket, and cricket has rules which it is the duty of an umpire to administer.

This England! These humourless Test matches and these excessive dutiful Dogberrys of the cricket field!

Still, despite the Griffin incident it was obvious that the crowd enjoyed the 'exhibition' game, so much so that I suggest that in future, to guarantee some share of public amusement on these occasions, the 'exhibition' game be played at the beginning, not the end, of the Test match proper.

Neville Cardus
National Liberal Club
London SW1

THROWING

SIR – If Mr P.G.H. Fender's idea that throwing should be made legal is adopted, may I recommend that a thrower should be allowed only a very limited run? My wife suggests the rhythm might be slow, slow, quick, quick, throw.

We both feel keenly about this, having just got back from Lord's.

H.C.S. Perry
Willingdon

11 AUGUST 1960

CRICKET THEN AND NOW

SIR – The game we call cricket can now, with safety, be described as quite different from that played 25 years ago. Finding Saturday free, for once, from other commitments, I visited the Oval for the first time this season to watch Middlesex score 69 for no wicket before lunch.

Surrey did their best with 40 overs, but their attack was more respectable than penetrative. W.E. Russell's share of the morning's two hours' excitement was 26 not out, on the ground where Hobbs could score a century before lunch.

Between 1934 and 1937 I regularly cycled 50 miles to see cricket at Trent Bridge and remember a day towards the end of that period when this same county, Middlesex, scored 525 for seven wickets, with centuries from Hendren, Price and Compton and 50 from Edrich, and that in the days before artificially shortened boundaries.

At the Oval on Saturday Middlesex accelerated to 284 for seven wickets before declaring to leave Surrey ten minutes' batting. It is not unkind to say that the county professional batsman is destroying his own livelihood by this dreary progress which no one will pay to see.

R.A. Hastings
London SW13

13 AUGUST 1960

MIDDLESEX'S TACTICS

SIR – Mr R.A. Hastings puts the responsibility for Middlesex's batting at the Oval last Saturday morning on two young professionals, ignoring incidentally the more eventful and, I think, not unentertaining part of the day's play which came later. He also does not appear to take into account that Gale and Russell may have been following my instructions as captain.

What the genuine lover of cricket rightly abhors most is purposeless cricket. The opening stand of Gale and Russell succeeded in its purpose, which was to lay a foundation and provide a springboard for an attack later when some excellent Surrey bowling was less accurate.

The attack was made, and we were able to declare, take two wickets that evening, and ultimately win by an innings, our first victory at the Oval for 12 years.

I do not suggest that whether we won or not was the only thing that mattered. The modern county captain has to be constantly alive to the need for entertaining the public, and I have always believed that the way one plays the game is more important than winning it. But it is part of the character of cricket that it is many-sided. If every ball were hit for six, it would be as dull as if no strokes were played at all.

Mr Hastings makes a comparison with a Middlesex performance in 1937 on a notoriously good batting wicket at Trent Bridge. If he had to compare that day with a present-day match, it would have been fairer and kinder to take the last match which Middlesex played at Trent Bridge, in August 1959.

In the day's play in 1937 (the second day) Middlesex scored at just over four runs an over. Last year the same young batsmen whom Mr Hastings now criticises initiated an assault on the first morning which produced 180 before lunch and averaged over five runs an over through the innings.

We won the match in 1959, but the one in 1937 ended in an aimless draw. After the boisterous batting last August I do not remember anyone writing to the newspapers expressing appreciation of the day's play or, for that matter, comparing it with a dull day in the 1930s.

John Warr
London NW8

19 AUGUST 1960

SIR – The weakness of Mr John Warr's case, I think, is that he fails to distinguish between batsmen genuinely laying a foundation and batsmen merely occupying the crease. An experienced watcher requires only five minutes to tell the difference.

At the Oval we saw batsmen playing every ball, good or bad, with equal respect. We saw, during the morning, languid running turning threes into twos, twos into ones, and a number of singles not attempted at all. Some county opening batsmen have always regarded the first hour at the wicket as acclimatisation time. There was a Warwickshire player who could safely be left for an hour while one took a walk round the ground.

What concerns many of us is that whole teams apparently now look on the opening two hours of a match in the same way, a private foundation-laying period which might well take place behind closed doors before the public are admitted. It is not encouraging to see two such experienced county captains as Mr Warr and Mr Marlar defending this practice.

I agree with Mr Warr that no one wants to see every ball hit for six. What we do not, obviously, agree on is the definition of 'purposeless cricket'.

R.A. Hastings
London SW13

23 AUGUST 1960
QUICK CENTURY

SIR – Reading Mr Swanton's reference to the late Mr E.R.T. Holmes's century in 65 minutes, I wondered whether that was the occasion I remember so well.

I used to be able sometimes to leave my office early and get to the Oval around five o'clock, after which hour one was admitted at half-price (6d). On one occasion Holmes made a century and Freddie Brown a double century, and altogether I saw more than 200 runs scored between five o'clock and 6.30. Not bad value for 6d.

D.W. Cay
London SE27

20 MAY 1961
1,000 IN MAY

SIR – Mr R.A. Roberts in 'Sporting Commentary' rightly remarks on the elusiveness of 1,000 runs in May and on the fact that only three players have accomplished this feat – the great W.G. in 1895, Wally Hammond in 1927 and Charlie Hallows in 1928.

Perhaps the spectacular way in which Hallows, the Lancashire lefthander, attained this figure may be of interest.

On the Wednesday morning, 30 May, Lancashire commenced a match with Sussex, and up to that date Hallows had scored 768 runs in the month. By the close of play he had scored 190 not out; on the following day he got the necessary 42 runs and was bowled next ball.

His innings were 100, 101, 51 not out, 123, 101 not out, 22, 74, 104, 58, 34 not out and 232, making 1,000 runs exactly and giving him an average of 125.00.

Cedric Adams
Redhill

23 MAY 1961

'E.M.'

SIR – I was interested in the article in *The Daily Telegraph* on E.M. Grace (against whom I remember playing about 60 years ago).

Other things that might have been mentioned are that he was a lob bowler, that he played many strokes with a cross bat (owing, it is said, to his having used a bat too big for him as a boy), and that he was probably the finest point the game has ever known.

T. Usher
Lord's Cricket Ground
London NW8

30 MAY 1961

BOWLED 'W.G.', CAUGHT 'E.M.'

SIR – Middlesex, playing against Gloucestershire at Lord's, found themselves batting on a decidedly sticky wicket. 'W.G.' bowled a ball just short of a length on the leg stump; it reared sharply, but A.E. Stoddart got well on top of it and played it down with a perfect defensive stroke.

'E.M.', however, had 'crept up' (a favourite manoeuvre of his) and took the ball practically off the face of Stoddart's bat with his right hand, transferred it to his left and handed it to the wicketkeeper – without either of them having moved their feet!

(Stoddart was reminded of the incident many years later, shortly before he died; he admitted that the incident still rankled, although he quite appreciated the humour of it!)

Royman Browne
Richmond

6 JUNE 1961

'E.M.'

SIR – I played against E.M. Grace on many occasions, chiefly at Lansdowne, Bath.

I was at a preparatory school at Clifton about 1890. The Australians came to play against Gloucestershire on the county ground at Bristol and we were taken to see the match.

During the game 'E.M.' was batting to Jones, the fast bowler, who was bumping them a great deal, and 'E.M.' did not like it; after each ball of the five in one over he flung his bat down the pitch and wrung his hands as if he had been rapped on the fingers.

After the last ball a man in the crowd shouted out some remark (I forget what it was) which pricked 'E.M.'; he left the wicket and ran off to get at the man, who when he saw him bowed out of the ground through the entrance gate, 'E.M.' after him.

'E.M.' was away about ten minutes and it was said that he chased the man a long way down into the town. He then returned and continued to bat. We boys were much annoyed at losing ten minutes' cricket.

What would happen nowadays if such a thing took place? In those days cricket was a real 'game' and full of fun and unreported incidents.

W.S. Medlicott
Hawick

13 JUNE 1961

E.M.'S CHANGE OF BOWLING

SIR – The letters you have published about E.M. Grace have been most amusing and interesting. I saw him many times captain the Thornbury side against Gloucester City on the 'Spa' ground.

Arthur Winterbottom, the Gloucester skipper, usually bet him £1 that he would not take five wickets (solely with the object of keeping him on).

On one occasion with the Gloucester score 210 for three a member of his side ventured a suggestion of a change at his end (he had bowled since the opening).

His reply was: 'A very good idea. I'll try the other end!'

He usually stored a large whisky and soda between the square leg umpire's legs and refreshed himself regularly between overs.

S.T. Freeman
Worcester

15 JUNE 1961

'E.M.'

SIR – Many years ago my father was present on the Bristol County Ground and told me of such an incident concerning Dr E.M. Grace and his apparently hurt fingers. He was then coroner for the lower division of Gloucestershire. The call, in a loud voice, which pricked him, was: 'Why doesn't hold an inquest on 'em?'

John L. Clapp
Ammore Dell

SIR – Mr W.S. Medlicott on his letter of 6 June records that as a boy he saw 'E.M.' when playing Ernest Jones, the Australian fast bowler, fling his bat down the pitch after each ball in one over and wring his hands as if he had been rapped on the knuckles.

I always understood that 'E.M.' let go of his bat whenever he thought that a kicking ball would rap his knuckles, and so avoided them being pinched against his bat. This would also, I presume, avoid being caught off one's gloves – unless 'E.M.' himself was fielding 'point'. He, of course, never wore gloves.

Mr P.J. Paravicini records that 'W.G.' always told the story how on a sticky wicket he caught Stoddart at point and handed the ball to the wicketkeeper, Frizzy Bush, without either of them moving a foot.

George Drummond
Mount Rule

17 JUNE 1961

'E.M.'

SIR – An uncle of mine who knew E.M. Grace told me 60 years ago of a local match at Downend near Bristol in which 'E.M.' was playing.

The umpire gave him 'out'. E.M.'s reaction was to shout indignantly: 'Out? Then out you go, out of my field!'

C.V. Burder
Brighton

24 JUNE 1961

'E.M.'

SIR – In justice to the memory of a cricketer I must suggest that Mr C.V. Burder's memory has failed him.

I well remember such an incident as the subject of a drawing by Raven Hill in *Punch* at just about the time Mr Burder mentions. I had no difficulty in turning it up, and found it in the issue of 20 June, 1900. The hero of the incident, needless to say, was not E.M. Grace, but a local farmer:

'Oh, hout be oi? Then hout you goes hout of my field!'

P.G. Hurst
Henfield

25 MAY 1961

CRICKET CATERING

SIR – If, as one assumes, the MCC and the various county cricket committees want to attract the public back to the game, they really must do something about the catering arrangements at the first-class grounds.

Lord's, which should be an example, is just about as bad as it could be in this respect. Prices are very high (in the Tavern the other day I paid 6s 5d for a pint of beer, a sad and almost meatless pork pie, a cheese sandwich and a hard-boiled egg) and service, where it exists at all, is extremely poor.

The Oval is a good deal better so far as catering goes, yet at the only bar on the west side of the ground, at 5.45 p.m. on the Saturday of the Australian match, one elderly, unhurried gentleman was dispensing drinks to a queue whose members showed most emotions between amused tolerance and ill-concealed fury.

If people can't get a glass of beer or a cup of tea and a piece of cake at reasonable cost and without performing a queuing marathon which will prevent them from seeing much of the cricket, they just won't bother to turn up at all.

A.C. Austin
South Chailey

11 JULY 1961

TENNIS VERSUS CRICKET

SIR – From 2.10 p.m. to 4.15 p.m. during last Thursday after-noon's play at Leeds in the third Test both TV channels gave themselves to lawn tennis, with the exception of seven minutes of cricket from the BBC.

Surely the idea of having two channels is to provide alterna-tive programmes? There are millions interested in each sport. All could easily be satisfied.

For the cricket enthusiasts to have two identical pictures of Wimbledon and no cricket is maddening. The fact that the men's events are only the equivalent of minor counties matches makes it no easier to bear.

Dr R.W. Cockshut
Chairman
Cricket Society
London WC2

14 JULY 1961

TENNIS VERSUS CRICKET

SIR – May I endorse Dr R.W. Cockshut's comments in your issue of 11 July? Viewers saw not one ball of the greatest spell of fast bowling in recent years, that of Trueman on Saturday.

With due respect to the ladies concerned, the tennis was of minor importance in comparison – particularly as England were certain to win, in any case, the tennis final.

One of your correspondents refers to the fact that Wimbledon can only be seen for ten days each year; Fred Trueman's bowling was something we may never see again!

John Leech
London WC1

17 JULY 1961

TENNIS VERSUS CRICKET

SIR – Surely Dr R.W. Cockshut, whose letter you published on 11 July, must realise that the divorce rate in this country would rise alarmingly should cricket be televised on one television channel and tennis on the other?

Morwenna Macneal
Campbeltown
Argyll

15 JULY 1961

WHY SO MUCH FUSS?

SIR – What a lot of nonsense is being written about Test-match wickets! Now Headingley is to be the subject of a boring post-mortem.

After all, the Test there did run three full days, and Cowdrey, Harvey, McDonald and Pullar at least showed that batsmen could get runs by judicious application.

Surely the extension of Test-match time to five days was the result of playing on doped dead wickets which used to be the fashion: wickets to break the bowler's heart and stifle the art of batsmanship! As soon as we have a pitch which gives some assistance to the bowler we have an outcry.

Have we forgotten that this game was invented to be played on grass? Now a 'grassy' wicket is to be abhorred, and consequently groundsmen shave the turf until the soil's natural protection is almost non-existent.

Benaud is credited with magnanimity and forbearance in saying that he is prepared to play on any wicket. It struck me as a simple statement of fact by a good sportsman.

Anyone who knows the game would rather see batsmen fighting for runs than a tiresome flow of easily-earned boundaries.

The thousands of club cricketers who play on an assortment of pitches week by week and never see a wicket of Test-match calibre except at long range must wonder what all the pother is about.

L.F. Gleig
Berwick-upon-Tweed

28 JULY 1961
CRICKET CHEWERS

SIR – I wonder if I am alone in suffering a feeling of disgust at the sight of Test cricketers indulging in the habit of chewing while playing the game.

Great cricketers of the past have managed to overcome the tenseness of batting in Test cricket without having to resort to a constant movement of the jaws, and one is tempted to assume that these gentlemen are simply lowering their standards of behaviour in common with so many other sections of the community.

The pity of it is that they are the heroes of the many schoolboys who watch them, and if the chewing habit is acceptable in Test-match circles what chance have we poor schoolmasters of maintaining standards on the cricket field? Unfortunately the first boys to fall for this fad are just the ones we are trying hardest to persuade to raise their standards of behaviour both on the field and off it.

P.G.C. Howard
Bungay Grammar School

5 AUGUST 1961

RICHIE BENAUD

SIR – A friend of mine sent a copy of Richie Benaud's book *Way of Cricket* to Old Trafford during the fourth Test match, explaining it was for a sick friend in hospital and requesting Benaud's autograph. The book was received back by return of post, duly autographed by the entire touring side, together with a 'Get-Well' card bearing the message: 'Wishing you a speedy recovery to Health and Happiness – Richie Benaud'.

Great cricketer and captain the man undoubtedly is. By such a simple personal gesture amid the worries of leading Australia in the crucial match of the Test series does he also show himself to be a gentleman in the truest sense.

N.A. Thompson
London SE19

19 AUGUST 1961

THREE MINUTES OUT

SIR – As at Old Trafford, again at the Oval, a Test match is being played by timepieces which differ by some two or three minutes from Greenwich 'pips' or Big Ben's chimes. This is perhaps a very minor irritation to spectators, viewers or listeners who find themselves robbed of an over through no fault of their own.

But is it not also a sign of the lazy administration of cricket in this country? When racecourses throughout the land can synchronise watches because of the importance of the 'off' to both bookmakers and bettors, one would think it reasonable to expect that advertised hours of play 11.30 to 6.30 should not mean 11.27 to 6.27.

Oliver Sandbach
Twickenham

11 SEPTEMBER 1963

PATTERN THAT IS GROTESQUE AND UNIQUE

SIR – Mr Rex Alston recommends that only one ball an innings be used in first-class cricket, as happens in school and club cricket, and he is kind enough to say he would like to know the views of your Cricket Correspondent. Over, in fact, to me.

Well, most of the captains would hate it, and four-fifths of their bowlers would hate it. Personally I should be delighted, and so in due course, I believe, would the crowds.

English cricket is in the grip of an insidious fetish, the 'props' of which are a grassy pitch, and squads of medium and fastish bowlers who use every available means to maintain and even improve the ball's original polish so that it will swing about and 'move off the seam' from dawn till dusk.

These tireless robots fire diligently away, putting the ball on the spot (just short of a length) while their captains enjoy a mental siesta, and the spectators a literal one. The batsmen spar about, and sooner or later give a catch to the wicket-keeper standing back, making way for someone else who bats in much the same way, and either comes to a similar end or, miscalculating slightly, pads up and is lbw not offering a stroke.

My picture may be a little far-fetched, but not very. Also I should honourably exclude certain counties, chief among them at the moment Gloucestershire, Worcestershire, Glamorgan and Yorkshire. English county cricket generally is conducted now according to a grotesque pattern which has absolutely no relevance anywhere else in the world. Hence the fact that we have won only one Test rubber abroad since 1954–55 and only three out of 12 major ones since the War. Unless variety and the opportunity for tactical manoeuvre can be restored the first-class game will grow ever more dreary and will command less support. That means the restoration of the slow bowler, whose art and guile must be nurtured by a captain who also uses his wits.

One ball an innings would force everyone's hand: but Mr Alston would have to arrange for a cramming establishment in the close season to instil principles which few of the present generation have had much chance of learning. Even so, it might be harder than ever for a while to get genuinely-finished matches, for slow bowlers, unlike fast ones, take time to nourish and mature.

This summer suddenly people are beginning to see just where English cricket has been led by current fashions in wicket preparation, team selection, and captaincy which together have formed an evil chain-reaction.

But at the best it must take a minimum of five years to get the game back into balance.

E.W. Swanton
Sandwich

SIR – There is a lot to be said for what Mr Rex Alston says, but I am not sure whether figures would support his suggestion for no new ball.

Considering all first-class innings up to 6 September, a fraction under 70 per cent never required the new ball at all this season, and something like a quarter of the remainder will hardly have needed one, and if so only to polish off the last wicket or two.

Rowland Bowen
Eastbourne

28 DECEMBER 1963
JACK HOBBS

SIR – The passing of Sir John (Jack) Hobbs has recalled a very pleasurable incident in the past.

At the Scarborough Cricket Festival in 1926 I invited Sir Jack and Lady Hobbs (then Mr and Mrs) to dine with me at the Grand Hotel, where only amateurs were then permitted to stay or dine. Arthur Gilligan, who was playing in the Festival (Gentleman that he is) told me that I was the first person ever to invite a professional cricketer there to dine and asked if he could, instead of dining with the amateurs, join us – which, of course, he did.

In March this year, when I wrote to Sir Jack on the occasion of Lady Hobbs's death, he wrote me as follows (omitting the formal parts):

'I remember quite well the occasion when you entertained my wife and self at the Grand Hotel, Scarborough, but I had forgotten that the Grand was out of bounds to professionals. What a change has arrived to professionals and amateurs nowadays.'

Joe W. Goldman
Egham

13 JUNE 1966

65 OVERS AS AN IMPETUS TO SCORING

SIR – I am sure that many regular readers of Monday Cricket Commentary could not help a quiet smile when Mr E.W. Swanton discussed my defence of the 65-over limitation on the grounds that it was merely 'theoretical argument'. Perhaps Mr Swanton could profitably browse through some old issues of *The Daily Telegraph* – Mondays preferably!

One of the most interesting features of the introduction of the 65-over limit has been the horrified and indignant reactions of the observers and critics. No doubt they would be very ready to complain when a game fizzles out into a draw with neither side having any real chance of bowling the other out. A splendid example of this type of cricket was the Manchester Test match of 1964 against Australia.

Mr Swanton will recall many pre-War county games in which this state of affairs existed. He will also, therefore, recall many occasions on which one side batted for a day and a half and the other occupied the crease for the remainder of the game. Were these contests living examples of the 'wit, originality and daring' of our forefathers, or could it be just another myth? At least present-day county cricket has a greater sense of urgency than this.

It is never an easy matter to finish games on good batting wickets between sides relatively evenly balanced. The 65-over limitation is a positive attempt to put sides into a position where there is a good chance of a result under these conditions. And look at the high number of results there have been!

Turning for a moment to a reply to my last letter by Mr A.J. Maynard, I would like to make a couple of points. He states that 'no amount of legislation will change a defensively minded batsman into an attacking one'. I beg to disagree. If a batsman is set a limited time to score a fairly high number of runs, he is under pressure to play shots and take risks. This happens invariably in county cricket on the third day, in the Gillette competition, and in most club cricket matches where time is very limited. The 65-over limitation is a logical extension of this fact.

Mr Swanton knows full well the difficulties of comparing games played under differing conditions. Therefore, I respectfully suggest that his examples (concerning total runs scored on the first day) quoted towards the end of his piece are fairly unimportant. Since then many high scores have been recorded in 65-over games. However, the bet is still available and the currency interests me very much.

O.S. Wheatley
Captain
Glamorgan County Cricket Club

24 JUNE 1966

LORD'S TEST

SIR – The uninhibited enthusiasm of the West Indies' supporters during the recent Test match at Lord's was indeed a sight for sore eyes.

It will, I hope, make for brighter cricket and also make it quite clear that neither is Lord's a cathedral, nor cricket a religious ceremony.

I sincerely hope that the apoplexy rate among sundry retired colonels and other *illuminati* was not on this occasion unduly excessive.

Joseph E. Cassidy
Barnet

8 AUGUST 1967

FAST BALL

SIR – Why have cricket writers and broadcasters taken in recent years to speaking of *quick* bowlers and bowling? In my schooldays and, I think, up to 1939 at least, bowlers not slow or medium were *fast*. One feels that Spofforth, Richardson, Gregory, Macdonald, Hitch, Larwood, *et al*, would have felt slightly undervalued to be called merely *quick*.

A cursory sampling of 1966 *Wisden* suggests that a category of *quick* bowlers is at yet unknown to the official cricket historians.

L.R.F. Earl
Croydon

12 AUGUST 1967

FAST BALL

SIR – Perhaps the answer to Mr L.R.F. Earl's query about the use of the word 'quick' by cricket writers and broadcasters is that they are using the word in the ecclesiastical sense – 'the quick and the dead'. If so, this is a distinction which sometimes needs to be made.

Geoffrey Griffiths
Atworth Vicarage

16 AUGUST 1967

BATSMAN'S DIFFICULTIES ON SLOW TURNER

SIR – I write in defence of cricketers who cannot answer back to those critics who take freedom to castigate the players in circumstances of which they (the critics) have no knowledge.

On 14 August, I was disgusted to read such twaddle as appeared in your paper (and in the *Guardian*) about the performances, on Saturday, of Barrington and Close.

Writers who have never played in a Test and who have no idea of the difficulties and responsibilities of the player in such a game should not be allowed to pontificate (and so mislead the reader) on a matter of which they know so little.

The first duty of a player in a Test is towards his side and its best interests. He is not there to pander either to the public or to the critics by fireworks at the expense of that duty.

Having bowled out their opponents for 140, and then having to bat on a wicket which has had '240 tons' of water on it, it was the duty of the batsmen to ensure, if they could, a total of about 300 to win the match, and that the methods employed to this end were what the captain approved was obvious. By what right do writers call such an effort 'tedious to death'? In the 'Verity Test' at Lord's Don Bradman showed what can happen to those who take the line advocated by critics, when on a 'slow turner'.

Only those who have played on such a wicket can know what pitfalls await a batsman who takes a chance for the sake of a little applause from such critics – you can easily be 'out' off a full toss (see Barrington's first over at Lord's) or off a long hop which 'stops'.

All batsmen like to score runs if they can reasonably do so – they do not refrain for the sake of annoying critics. It is just not playing the game to slang a man who cannot answer back if he has put up the shutters in the interests of his side (and with the approval of his captain on the spot).

I am no advocate of slow batting, but there are times when the demands of the situation and the interests of the side make it necessary, and critics should understand this.

Percy G.H. Fender
London W1

16 AUGUST 1967

STONEWALLING

SIR – Never since the noted stonewalling in Test cricket by Trevor Bailey have I so wished for an England player to be dismissed as I did Ken Barrington on Saturday.

Ida Jamieson
London SE13

19 AUGUST 1967

VARIATIONS IN ENGLAND'S SPORTING LORE

SIR – No one would presume to question the right of such a great cricketer and exponent of the game as Mr Percy Fender to 'pontificate' (as he puts it) on such a subject, whereas others 'who have not played in a Test' are told they are guilty of 'twaddle' if, in the manner of your excellent article, they criticise last Saturday's batting in the Test match and Mr Barrington's century in six and a half hours.

There was once a time when anything that was 'not cricket' was called 'unsporting'. Now we have to learn that something which really is 'cricket' need have no element of sportsmanship. *Autres temps, autres maurs.* It seems a pity!

Ernest Goodman Roberts
London SW1

UNCONVENTIONAL CRITIC

SIR – Most cricket lovers of my generation will vividly recall Mr P.G.H. Fender as the permanent wearer of an outsize sweater, as the inspiring if somewhat unconventional captain of the Surrey side during the 1920s, as a bowler of leg breaks, which were occasionally most effective, and as a hard-hitting but unorthodox batsman who once scored 113 runs in 42 minutes. It is therefore slightly ironic that he of all people should be 'disgusted' at the 'twaddle' written in *The Daily Telegraph* and the *Guardian* about the slow batting of Messrs Barrington and Close in the recent Test match at Trent Bridge.

While he is quite right to say (and here I fancy Messrs Swanton and Rowbotham would agree with him) that 'there are times when the demands of the situation and the interests of the side make slow batting necessary', the point at issue is whether or not such tactics were justified last Saturday. Mr Fender is entitled to disagree with the majority of critics, but I wonder what he would have said in his captaincy days had Sandham, however intolerable the circumstances, batted for seven hours for 109.

Mr Fender's strong feelings on the matter have driven him to write something precious near 'twaddle' himself. 'Writers who have never played in a Test should not be allowed to pontificate on a matter of which they know so little'. So presumably John Arlott must be forcibly gagged; E.W. Swanton, John Woodcock and their colleagues must submit their reports to censorship. As for Sir Neville Cardus, since he has neither played in a Test match nor (so far as I know) composed a symphony, on Mr Fender's argument he will have to give up writing about either cricket or music.

Gervase Hughes
London W8

GOODWILL ENDANGERED

SIR – Mr P.G.H. Fender (may his sweater never grow shorter) in his letter to you seems to me to miss the point. If first-class cricket is merely a matter of statistics – so many matches won or lost, so many runs scored – then England's innings in the last Test is all well and good. As far as the public was concerned, however, it simply wasn't worth the price of admission.

There exists a very great deal of goodwill towards the game, but players and captains, with the honourable exception of Sussex, seem determined to stifle it.

Trevor Frowd
Bovington

COMPTON'S COMMENT

SIR – If Mr P.G.H. Fender thinks that only ex-Test cricketers should be allowed to comment on the performances of Test players, he should have heard what Mr Denis Compton, who has played in more Test matches than even Mr Fender, said on television about Ken Barrington's batting on Saturday.

E. Rushton
Grange-over-Sands

22 AUGUST 1967

CONDEMNATION BY EMINENT CRICKETERS

SIR – Mr Percy Fender, the old Surrey captain, who was not, I believe, at Trent Bridge, justifies Ken Barrington's innings of 109 in nearly seven hours and says that neither I (who, by the way, was present) nor anyone else who has not played in a Test match is qualified to criticise it.

The proposition that the opinion of a critic who may have spent a lifetime with his subject is valueless unless he has practised it at the highest level is not one which many writers would accept. The pros and cons of such an argument could hardly be covered in a letter.

The fact, however, in this case is that there were many eminent Test cricketers at Trent Bridge, and all of them whose job was to write or broadcast about the game condemned the slow England batting, which, of course, centred on Barrington's innings. Most of them used language a good deal stronger than mine.

One who saw it through, in his capacity as selector, was Alec Bedser. If Mr Fender would accept his opinion I am sure that Mr Bedser would oblige him – in confidence, of course.

Mr Barrington has many virtues, to which I have often called attention. He can also be very tedious, restricting his strokes in a way which to the cricketing onlooker is not justified either by the bowling or by the state of the pitch.

No one wants to see a cricketer 'pander either to the public or to the critics' at the expense of his side. What is demanded of him is that he shall play the game in a positive and intelligent way. In this sense the professional cricketer is an entertainer, and if he cannot satisfy his audience, in the same way as an actor or any other artist, the house will soon be empty and he will be out of a job.

The crisis in English cricket at the moment lies in the example at the top. More people play than ever before. There is enormous affection for the game, seeking an outlet among people of all ages and walks of life.

In this age of ball-by-ball commentaries and wide television coverage Test matches are the centrepiece, and what happens therein will be followed and copied for better or for worse, right down the scale. If for no other reason, then it surely is the duty of the cricket writer to give as accurate an appraisal as he can.

Those who remember Mr Fender's mode of play in the 1920s must have been surprised at the naïve comment: 'You can easily be out off a full toss'. One can be out off anything, but to infer that on a 'slow turner' it is dangerous to hit full pitches is, to borrow his own phrase, twaddle.

E.W. Swanton
Sandwich

THE RISK

SIR – I was worried that Close might send in Barrington to score the three winning runs. We would then have had a draw.

W.D. Vercoe
Weston-super-Mare

23 AUGUST 1967
CRITICS & PLAYERS

SIR – The five letters which you printed on 19 August concerning my letter of 16 August to you are quite interesting, from some points of view, but none of the writers seem to have read, or remembered, the first paragraph of that letter.

They have taken up the cudgels with me over something which I was *very* careful not to write.

I did not write that critics should not criticise. Of course they should; that is what they are paid for. But I *did* say that in the course of their crits they should not castigate or pillory an individual player for doing what his captain, on the field, wishes or instructs him to do, and this the more especially in circumstances where the player cannot answer back; and I do not retreat from that position.

Perhaps I may be allowed to add that I have received many more letters than five (and *very* many more verbal expressions of opinion) supporting what I wrote.

Percy G.H. Fender
London W1

31 AUGUST 1968
MILLIONS SAW TEST INNINGS AT THE OVAL

From Mr J.P. Eddy QC

SIR – With all due respect to your esteemed contributor, Mr E.W. Swanton (29 August), the business of the MCC selectors was not to throw a bridge between the divided sporting communities of South Africa. It was to select the best available team to make the trip to South Africa, irrespective of any other considerations, political or otherwise.

Personally – and I am uninfluenced by the fact that I am a member of the MCC as well as a Worcestershire man – I have no doubt that the selectors addressed themselves exclusively to this task.

My feeling is, however, that in the case of Basil d'Oliveira they failed to give proper effect to the really decisive evidence.

One assumes that they judged him primarily on his form in the West Indies, and on this season's county matches. They should have judged him on his form at the Oval when, as millions of people saw for themselves on television, he proved himself to be an outstanding player at Test level.

Mr Swanton says that if justice has been done it has scarcely been seen to be done. As to that I would say that this is one of the few occasions when members of the public are able as eye-witnesses to judge for themselves whether justice has or has not been done, and there can be little doubt what their verdict is.

The decision of the selectors should be reconsidered, and the injustice which has unwittingly been done should be righted, even though it involves the sending of a larger party to South Africa than was originally intended.

J.P. Eddy
The Temple

UNCONVINCING REASONS

SIR – All prejudiced cricket lovers, and indeed many another, will have been saddened by the omission of d'Oliveira from the team to tour South Africa, and most of them will be quite unconvinced by the reasons given.

It is always desirable that the truth should look like the truth, but in this case, and for a variety of reasons, it looks nothing like it, and inevitably there will be those like myself who regard the assertions and denials of Mr Insole as diplomatic ones.

We shall choose to believe that the honest course would have been to tell d'Oliveira that he was omitted not on the score of ability, but partly to spare him the humiliations and indignities which he might well encounter and from which it would be difficult to shield him, and partly to spare the MCC embarrassment.

What a pity that the MCC did not refuse in the first place to have any truck with the matter of a tour in a country where racial discrimination is so rampant and cruel. But such a consummation would have been too much to expect.

Commercial interests are much too important, while double talk and expediency, never complete strangers to public life, are today common currency therein.

The good name of the MCC is, in the eyes of very many, tarnished and it seems to me not unjustly. As for the Selection Committee, they should resign and make way for another whether they were willing or unwilling parties to what will always appear a squalid episode; in either case there would be good reason for their action.

S.F. Marwood
Clifton

IN SOUTH AFRICA

SIR – Amid the spate of criticism which predictably has descended on the heads of the MCC Selection Committee for omitting Basil d'Oliveira from the England party to tour South Africa, one overriding factor appears to have been completely overlooked.

Had d'Oliveira been selected, the tensions to which he would have been subjected might well have had a serious effect on his play as to place the England team at a serious disadvantage in the Test matches.

The MCC have stated that in selecting the team they were motivated by cricketing considerations only and that their objective was to pick the best team to beat South Africa in South Africa.

May it not be that that statement is not only wholly truthful, but that the MCC officials are perhaps a little wiser than their critics.

R.E. Palmer
Gerrards Cross

2 SEPTEMBER 1968
DOUBT THROWN ON WORD

From Lord Fisher of Lambeth

SIR – Speaking in your leader of 29 August of the non-selection of Basil d'Oliveira, you conclude that the MCC appears to have bowed to non-existent pressures, and that if it did, it should bow again in shame.

But the selectors have said explicitly (and you quote their words) that they acted solely on their duty to select the best possible team from a cricketing point of view for the MCC tour of South Africa.

In your conclusion you appear to cast doubt upon the word of the selectors and to have bowed to the pressure of other considerations. If so, should you not bow again in shame?

Fisher of Lambeth
Sherborne

4 SEPTEMBER 1968
CONNECTED EVENTS?

SIR – I am very sad that Basil d'Oliveira will not be touring South Africa this winter, but I am equally sad and extremely annoyed that I was prevented from seeing that even greater

Test cricketer Colin Bland in action at the weekend for the Rest of the World XI.

The Trades Union Congress chiefs and Labour MPs who are so concerned about d'Oliveira may not realise that there may be some connection between the two events.

For the selectors (not MCC) to have picked d'Oliveira would obviously have invited reprisals from the South Africans leading to the cancellation of the tour. This was not worth risking on what would have been a border-line choice.

The selectors might completely reject my theory. If so I can only say that they should have had it clearly in their minds that a South African Test cricketer had recently been insulted by the British Government.

L.H. Giggins
Oxted

7 SEPTEMBER 1968
IRISH SOUND

SIR – I find it somewhat satisfying to know that, despite the clamour of press and television, there is in my office a young lady who thinks that d'Oliveira is the President of Eire.

A.M. Greig
Teddington

11 SEPTEMBER 1968
APARTHEID
From Brigadier C.E. Lucas Phillips

SIR – I suggest that the Reverend David Sheppard and those who think like him about racial segregation on the South African cricket field would be fulfilling their Christian mission more effectively if they were to direct their zeal to the far more vicious forms of apartheid practised in the Sudan, Zanzibar, India, Abyssinia, Guyana, Nigeria, Kenya, Egypt and other countries.

The pale discrimination of South Africa fades into insignificance when compared with the bloodshed, persecution, callous neglect and frequently wholesale massacres that occur in such territories from racial, religious, caste and tribal discriminations.

Is it nothing to Christian churchmen that the black, brown and yellow people slaughter and persecute one another? Are the trivialities of cricket of greater moment than the mass killing of Negroes by Arabs? Have we come to the pass that we must include a coloured man in an English team because he is coloured?

If d'Oliveira had not been a coloured person, no one would have seriously criticised the MCC. No one has made a fuss about the equally unfortunate Milburn.

C.E. Lucas Phillips
Oxshott

12 SEPTEMBER 1968
WORLD CRISIS

SIR – Ought not the duty of selecting touring cricket teams to be transferred from the MCC to the United Nations?

L.G. Duke
London W8

20 SEPTEMBER 1968

SOUTH AFRICA FORCED D'OLIVEIRA ISSUE

SIR – Your leading article of 18 September accuses me of 'wanting to imbue sport with politics'.

I would not have thought that any serious observer would have failed to notice that all sport in South Africa is controlled by politics. It was South Africa which introduced politics into sport, and forces, for example, an English cricket team, if it visits the country, to play against an all-white team in front of segregated crowds.

Mr E.W. Swanton wrote on your front page, also on 18 September, that d'Oliveira had been 'deprived by their own political system from playing for the land of his birth'. Under-lying your comment is the attitude that life can all be kept in separate compartments – cricket, politics, religion . . . in a kind of mental apartheid.

It was obvious from the moment d'Oliveira first played for England in 1966 that selection for the next South African tour would impinge on what is probably the most important issue in the world today, that of race relations. The way this was presented to the public was of the greatest possible importance. This is why the political side should have been cleared up by the MCC Committee before the English cricket season began. Instead, matters were allowed to slide until all depended on the selection or non-selection of a player they regarded as border-line.

As for 'fanning hostility between Britain and South Africa', I am concerned not only about our relations with white South Africans, but with the great majority of South Africans, who are not white. The greatest cricketing tragedy is that 28,000 non-white cricketers in South Africa can never be considered for any representative teams.

David Sheppard
London E16

WHERE BLAME LIES

SIR – Congratulations on your leader 'No Play' (18 September). This was one of the few articles that put the blame squarely where it belongs – on both sides.

Would it be too late, or too degrading, for us to apologise for our part in this fiasco, and ask if after all we could play South Africa at cricket (and not politics), at the same time giving Mr Vorster free leave and encouragement to boot out any reporter or clergyman who so much as mentions politics?

If the political 'sportsmen' in this country think that this approach might in any way be condoning South Africa's policies, they could always send a separate letter confirming our disapproval of apartheid, but I suspect that Mr Vorster may already be aware of this.

D.P.J. Lloyd
Fareham

EPISCOPAL ADVICE

SIR – It is reported that, before accepting the task of leading the MCC team to tour South Africa, Colin Cowdrey asked the Bishop of Coventry for his advice.

Would the Reverend David Sheppard let us know if he thought to consult his Bishop before his handling of a situation which may lead to the dismay of cricketers in South Africa and our own country.

C.A. Wallington
St Stephen's Vicarage

21 SEPTEMBER 1968

FOUR CULPRITS IN D'OLIVEIRA AFFAIR

SIR – Only one of the five parties involved in the d'Oliveira business – Dolly himself – has come out with any credit. The other four have displayed remarkable standards of twittishness.

First, the MCC, having rejected a player for reasons of (in) ability, should have stood their ground and not allowed themselves to be stampeded by witch-hunting clerics (for few people really believe that the rejection was based on colour).

Secondly, the role of David Sheppard in imputing racialism to the MCC was rather nauseating; I got the distinct impression that he was determined to find a colour bar come what may. Thirdly, Mr Vorster's pathetic hate in splitting mankind into 4d and 5d packets is loathsome and abhorrent.

But it is probably the fourth twittishness which takes the biscuit; Mr Denis Howell regretted the entry of politics into sport, but it was precisely his mates who injected a full dose of politics into sport when they as good as put a veto on meetings between Britons and Rhodesians on the cricket pitch. There may be some measure of poetic justice in Mr Vorster's veto towards the MCC.

One thing is inescapable: when people stir up racial trouble, whether they be pro or anti, they sow continuing seeds of misery and discontent. An active catalyst in such matters is the Race Relations Act.

W.F. Shepherd
Tunbridge Wells

24 SEPTEMBER 1968

CAVALIERS' EXAMPLE

SIR – In his studied rudeness to the integrity of the MCC, Mr Vorster has surely reached the height of hypocrisy. In the recent matches of the International Cavaliers and the Rest of the World elevens, white South Africans have played with, and against, coloured cricketers. So we must assume that Mr Vorster has no objection to mixed cricket provided it does not take place in South Africa, and that the objection to such mixed cricket comes not from South African players but from politicians.

I hope that the MCC will stick to their guns and call the tour off. I hope also that they will ask the Australian and New Zealand cricketing authorities to boycott tours of South Africa, while making it abundantly clear that cricketers, white or black, from South Africa will always be welcome in our countries. When the cricket-loving people of South Africa find that they have to travel abroad to see their team playing worthwhile opposition, perhaps they can make their protests felt in the place that matters most – the ballot box.

H.A. Mould
West Kirby

28 SEPTEMBER 1968
TEST TEAMS

SIR – Now that the MCC tour to South Africa appears to be off, perhaps this might be the time to look into the future and see what the composition of an XI to represent England in Test matches could be.

With the increasing number of non-English players now participating in county cricket, many of whom have not represented their country of origin in Test matches and presumably therefore eligible to play for England, perhaps there could come a time in the not too distant future when we might see an England XI without an Englishman.

R. Glover-Wright
Stanmore

6 SEPTEMBER 1968
SOBERS AGAIN

SIR – Gary Sobers's recent feat of scoring a six off each ball of an over recalls an earlier, less publicised record achieved by Sobers when playing for E.W. Swanton's Commonwealth XI against Malaysia at Kuala Lumpur in March 1964.

On this occasion he dismissed five batsmen with five consecutive balls, the last three of one over and the first two of his next.

If memory serves me aright, we spectators had earlier that day been treated to the unusual sight of the great man being dismissed for 0 by Dr A.E. Delilkan, the Malaysian leg-break bowler.

J. Sharples
Haywards Heath

26 MAY 1969
SUNDAY CRICKET

SIR – Cricket with restricted overs and its own laws as played in the Gillette Cup and in the Sunday League may be good entertainment but is certainly not the game of cricket. We need a new name – may I suggest 'cricketette'?

C.I. Langford
Reigate

7 JUNE 1969
FRANK WOOLLEY

SIR – Miss Dorothea St Hill Bourne's tribute to Frank Woolley (29 May) prompts me to recall that when I was first a student, in Wales, I was sent to preach in the church of a rather staid and strict community not far from Builth Wells.

The Englishman always felt at a disadvantage in a Welsh pulpit, so any telling illustration seemed heaven sent. Touching on the theme of 'Heaven', as I had been bidden to do, and not wishing unduly to depress my congregation (or to display my own ignorance of that subject), I gaily suggested that in my native county a Kentish schoolboy's idea of heaven was August Bank Holiday on the St Lawrence Cricket Ground at Canterbury, a bag of late cherries and Frank Woolley about to complete his century.

Unfortunately for me the elders in 'the big seat' were not amused, so the congregation remained glum. It was duly reported to the Reverend Principal, who suggested over an admirable cup of tea that I suppress my tendency to levity. But the good man poured forth a eulogistic tribute to our hero Frank Woolley, deploring that he had not managed to play for Glamorgan.

May I add that years later, during the grim days Margate experienced in England's front line, Frank Woolley's influence counted for much among the troops there, as I had good reason to know. Even then he was playing 'with a straight bat', bless him.

Victor Downs
Old Heathfield Vicarage
Sussex

4 JULY 1969

THE CHANGING NATURE OF SUNDAY CRICKET

SIR – It is possible to extenuate without making excuses and while I yielded to no one in my admiration for Hobbs, Mead, Woolley and Hendren, whom I saw with pleasure both before and after the First World War, I do think that Mr E.W. Swanton might have mentioned that the circumstances under which they played were different from those pertaining today.

In their time Sunday cricket did not occur and some of them, at least, were regular church-goers. Now what Mrs Proudie was pleased to call 'Sabbath Day observance' has largely faded and there is great commercial pressure on players to indulge in Sunday cricket.

The whole game with the introduction of highly paid overseas players has become much more gladiatorial than it was in the days of my youth. While I was playing club cricket in West Sussex in the Twenties and early Thirties, we had three capped county players who had been born in our small town, and the next village also had three, one of whom played for England – and we were not unique in the Sussex of those days. This added much to the friendly atmosphere of the game and we shall not recover that atmosphere in this commercial age, nor shall we recover some of the high cricket ideals of the past in the present climate.

I have had much enjoyment from playing relaxed Sunday cricket myself, regarding it as something of an antidote to the high-pressure commercialised world. Now that Sunday cricket also has been partly commercialised, trouble has arisen from which so far Tom Graveney is the only scapegoat.

G.H. Jennings
Bushey Heath

31 JULY 1969

ILLINGWORTH AS CAPTAIN OF TEST TEAM

SIR – As a county captain of considerable experience and a former Test selector of a vintage era, I would like to congratulate the England Test selectors on the selection of Ray Illingworth as the captain of England, and furthermore to pay tribute to his extremely skilful handling of an England side which had its share of selection problems. The choice of Illingworth as the England captain met with approval in the county dressing-rooms at the outset, and I have a profound respect for first-class players' opinions.

I am persuaded to make these comments because of Mr E.W. Swanton's reluctance to recognise the skills of this fine player and furthermore his inability to recognise the virtues of any captain of England who does not come from Oxbridge. It is fortunate indeed that history will record its own appreciation in due course.

Wilfred Wooller

Secretary
Glamorgan County Cricket Club

E.W. Swanton writes: As the surviving author of the standard work it interests me that Mr Wooller can predict with such assurance the verdict of history. One applauds modern cricket and cricketers (irrespective of their origins) where one can, but I take the job of the critic to be to interpret the modern game to his readers as best he can, and to show it in perspective. Ray Illingworth as a player and captain has many virtues, often underlined by me; but the batting of the England XI this summer, under his tactical direction, has been some of the slowest of all time, and whether such a state of affairs is justified by circumstances may be easier to judge by spectators on the spot than by a county secretary, even of such impressive credentials, sitting in his office in Cardiff.

14 AUGUST 1969

LESSONS IN BATTING

SIR – May I, as a 'watcher' of cricket, join in the Wooller versus Swanton correspondence?

At the outset let me say that Mr Swanton is, undoubtedly, the best cricket correspondent in the world. However, I am

amazed that he should think that English batsmen need to be
given lessons in tactical batting by their captain. If such is the
case they have no right to be in the England team. Ray Illingworth has shown, thus far, that he is England's most successful
captain since Len Hutton – a fact, I trust, the selectors will not
overlook when making their appointment for the forthcoming
tour of Australia.

I had the pleasure of playing with Ray Illingworth during
National Service and I certainly didn't expect him to show me
how to bat – I knew – if I hadn't I should not have played.

No, Mr Swanton, if there is any blame, and I don't necessarily accept the fact, it should be laid fairly and squarely
where it belongs: on the shoulders of the batsmen, not on the
English captain who, whether batting, bowling or fielding, has
set a supreme example to his men.

A.E. Stallard
Liverpool

E.W. Swanton writes: I only meant that it is up to the captain to
sketch the general tactical plan of his side's innings.

23 AUGUST 1969

LIGHT-METERS FOR CRICKET

SIR – Proposals have been repeatedly made this cricket season
for the use of light-meters to judge whether play is, or is not,
feasible.

There are two fundamental objections to light-meters
being used for this purpose. One is that light-meters *only*
measure active light, and any photographer who has ever
used a light-meter knows only too well how often his eyes
tell him the light is all right but his light-meter says it is not.
Thus the light-meter is of no value in helping to judge

whether the light is suitable from the point of view of the human eye.

The other even more serious objection is that the human eye's reaction to light is extraordinarily subjective. That is to say, a sudden dark cloud on a bright day can produce an effect of gloom on the human eye which (and especially if the cloud is quite local as is often the case) may not even be measurable on a light-meter. Conversely, if the light is poor at the start of play, play may often continue (provided it gets no worse) in conditions which, if they arose during an otherwise bright day, would be regarded as impossible.

This has nothing to do with background, buildings or anything else; simply, the highly subjective manner in which light affects the human eye, the clue of course being the infinitely variable expansion and contraction of the pupil of the eye. Older readers will recall the way in which Sir Donald Bradman used always to walk slowly to the wicket to enable his eyes to accustom themselves to the different quality of the light on the field from what it was in the pavilion; his custom illustrates perfectly the way the human eye adapts itself – and takes a little time to do so, too.

R. Bowen
Eastbourne

29 JULY 1970

BEST COMMENTATOR
From Major-General R.K. Exham

SIR – I was very disappointed that the first three Test matches against The Rest of the World were not televised. Presumably this was because Wimbledon, The Open Golf Championship and the Commonwealth Games filled the programme.

Instead I listened to the radio and was most impressed by their team of commentators – Brian Johnston, John Arlott,

Alan Gibson and Trevor Bailey. I have left out one name, Richie Benaud. This great Australian cricketer is, I think, the best of them all. He is outstanding in all departments of the game, and what he says is always interesting.

However, what I so like is his oft-repeated remark, 'It reminds me of . . .' This is followed by some delightful story of an incident in a past Test match in which he played, or some other interesting point about cricket which he remembers. He is, of course, an expert on the laws of the game.

I wonder if other cricket lovers regard Richie Benaud as I do.

R.K. Exham
Woking
Surrey

20 FEBRUARY 1971

STRAIN OF THE SEVEN-TEST TOUR

SIR – While I do not condone in any way the attitude of the English cricketers during the seventh Test match in Sydney, I think that your leader (15 February) tends to look at the bumper incident in isolation without examining the underlying reasons for some of the regrettable incidents that have occurred on the tour.

Normally rational, phlegmatic cricketers like Boycott and Illingworth have behaved in a way alien to them primarily because of the tremendous mental and physical strains imposed on them by the demanding tour itinerary, which has crammed six Test matches into a very short space of time.

This was clearly an error by those who planned the tour, which has resulted in players being chosen despite doubts over their fitness and the selectors sometimes wondering whether they would in fact be able to choose a team. Test match has followed Test match with hardly a break allowing no time for recovery, physical or mental.

Other aggravating factors account for the present atmosphere. There have been several bad decisions by the umpires, nearly all in Australia's favour, which have been revealed by the television cameras. This has resulted in a general loss of confidence in the umpires which finally surfaced after the Snow bumper incident.

On top of this the attitude of the crowd throughout the series with their beer-can madness has increased the hostility between the countries. Boycott's bat-throwing incident was lamentable but no worse than the refusal of certain leading batsmen to 'walk' until given out by the umpire.

The sooner the Ashes are buried for good, the better.

T.N. Costley-White
Cheltenham

24 JUNE 1972

SPIN BOWLING

SIR – How one applauds Mr E.W. Swanton's support (20 June) for the plea of the England captain for more spin bowling in limited-over cricket! But such support and such a plea should be taken up at all levels of the game. The absence of good spin bowling is detrimental to all, the ordinary game as well as the first-class game.

It is a problem fostered in the schools by coaches and by boys of having to go through the ritual, often with an old ball, of beginning every innings with two bowlers who run to the wicket – they often stand still when they get there – and eventually replacing them by two who run but a little less to the wicket.

Between them these four sometimes get the wickets because they get the chance and the practice and the confidence accrues from them. If they do not, it is an imaginative boy who will risk bowling a spinner. Where so-called speed has failed how will he succeed? Because the spin bowler needs as much practice in the middle as any, but he never gets the real grounding demanded and the gap between him and those who run to the wicket is made wider and wider.

Robert Avery
Marlborough College
Wiltshire

15 MAY 1977

THE SACKING OF TONY GREIG

SIR – The Cricket Council's decision to strip Tony Greig of the England captaincy must rank as one of the most unfortunate cricket decisions for some time – unfortunate that is for England, who before then entered the season with one of their greatest chances ever of decidedly defeating their great rivals, Australia, in the coming Test series.

Under Greig's mercurial leadership an exciting, talented and experienced team of great potential – possessing that magical ingredient of team spirit – has emerged. In Greig's own words, every one of England's cricketers who toured India and Australia last winter would have walked under a bus for him; I wonder how long it will be now before another captain can induce such loyalty and devotion?

Cricket lovers like me will sympathise with Greig's desire to improve the rewards to professional cricketers. We may not necessarily condone his methods but we freely recognise that his motives were certainly not to damage the game or destroy the spirit of Test cricket, to both of which he has personally contributed so much.

Why, oh why, couldn't the CC have saved their face, and England's chances, by reprimanding Greig, extracting a promise to take no further immediate action in the matter of the cricket 'circus', and suspending a decision until after the International

Cricket Conference has met, by which time the emotional element in any decision would be diluted?

Alan Edge
Leamington Spa

17 MAY 1977

FEATS FOR SUSSEX

SIR – How refreshing to find you, in your leader of 11 May, ignoring the premature judgments of the cricket establishment commentators and writers and coming out in support of Packer's buccaneering idea for a super-cricket competition.

Typical of the ill-informed comments was that by Henry Blofeld on ITV when he said that 'Greig came from South Africa little thought-of, and owed all his progress to Sussex CCC'!

As a long-time member of Sussex, and a born and bred supporter, I would in fairness to Greig point out that in his first season he scored a century (156) in his first county innings and totalled nearly 1,300 runs in the championship averages, while he took 63 wickets and his fielding was superb. His batting style was largely responsible for Sussex being the fastest run-getters in 1967.

Hardly a novice! Since then Sussex and England have been the main beneficiaries of his competitive approach to all aspects of the game, and I doubt if Sussex did more than tend to curb his natural aggressive style of batting to suit the three-day game.

S.W.H. Thompson
Warblington

PLAYERS' INCOMES

SIR – A young county cricketer who gets £2,500 (frequently substantially more) for doing the thing he loves for five months a year can scarcely be said to be underpaid. Most cricketers have 'regular' jobs which bring them in at least as much again.

Moreover, after perhaps ten years' service, they may expect a benefit which will bring them in a further £10,000. Not riches compared with other sports, but then cricket doesn't have such a great following.

For the superstars, contracting to go into the circus business for yet more money, to claim that they are doing this for the benefit of their less well-paid colleagues is loathsomely hypocritical and the opposite of the truth. The game would be harmed irreparably.

Peter Jackson
Shirley

CHOOSING A CAPTAIN

SIR – It seems to me to be a painfully cruel indictment of the state of English cricket administration when the future captain of our national side will be appointed because he is *not* one of the world's best players.

Richard Sutcliffe
Southport

NOT CRICKET
From Major-General E.A.E. Tremlett

SIR – Whatever the proposed international circus intend to call themselves, it will not be cricket they play.

E. Tremlett
Exeter

31 MAY 1977

ALL-ROUNDERS

SIR – In his commemoration of the 80th birthday of the peerless Frank Woolley, Mr E.W. Swanton omits the name of Dr W.G. Grace from his three outstanding all-round cricketers. This is heresy.

D.P. Smith
London SW1

6 AUGUST 1977

THE ANTI-PACKER ONSLAUGHT

SIR – Is it cricket, that time-honoured simile for fair play, for your cricket correspondents to assault verbally, day after day, the signatories of Packer contracts?

They are furious with Greig, weep for Underwood and Knott, show an unbecoming eagerness to detect hissing of the renegade gentlemen ('or are they players'?). Am I alone among cricket lovers in thinking it is time someone wrote in defence of those whose skill has given pleasure to millions?

Firstly, then, your cricket correspondents should remind themselves as well as their colleagues on other newspapers (Packer has been a unifying influence) that they are sports writers and not defence correspondents. An Englishman in no way betrays his country by seeking legitimate financial reward for outstanding talent. And that goes for nationals of other countries, too.

Secondly, most cricket spectators will have heard for the first time of the low salaries paid to county cricketers. If it has done nothing else the Packer 'intervention' has shed daylight on cricket finances.

Do we pay enough at the gates, especially for one-day matches? Do we pay enough in subscription fees? Sussex charges an annual £6.50 for out-of-county members. Kent charges £13.50 for in-county members. This enables two people to attend almost all matches, sit in the members' stand, take a car into the grounds.

Aren't we getting cricket on the cheap at the expense of those whom we go to see? Charges could be raised, even with concessions to old-age pensioners, provided cricket clubs continue to supply the excitement of 'star' players.

Marjorie Seldon
Sevenoaks

11 AUGUST 1977
CRICKET AND COUNTRY

SIR – I disagree entirely with Mrs Marjorie Seldon (6 August) who alleges that your cricket writers 'assault verbally, day after day, the signatories of Packer contracts'.

No one underestimates the talents of the 'renegade' players, and tributes are paid where they are due. Nevertheless, talent is only one side of the issue. There is also the question of loyalty to country and clubs to which they undoubtedly owe so much for their present status at the top.

As Test players they acquire various monetary and material assets over and above their salaries.

Any player who chooses to sell his birthright for a mess of pottage cannot really expect to escape public criticism.

E.M. Nerval
London SW15

WHEN CRICKETERS ARE AT LOGGERHEADS

SIR – The present cricket controversy to some extent echoes the past.

Although time has blurred the edges, today's rumpus appears to be only marginally different from the schism visited on the All England XI which William Clarke put on the road in 1846. It was at once popular and prosperous. It included all the stars of the day and, over the next three seasons, pitched its wickets at some 40 different venues up and down the country.

On the evidence of Dr Grace, Clarke, 'like most successful men, was a bit arbitrary'. He was 'disinclined to accept changes which did not accord with his own views or which might undermine his overall authority'. Thus six years later, in 1852, the breakaway United England XI came into being. Then, as now, some of the best-known players changed their allegiance – although one or two subsequently had second thoughts.

To play for the United England XI required an undertaking not to take part in any match which bore Clarke's *imprimatur*. But, cricket being what it is, within three years the two sides were playing together at Lord's for the benefit of the Cricketers' Fund, newly created to help those who had fallen on bad times.

From this one may be strengthened in the view that cricket will always be bigger than those, however famous, who play it; and that, whatever hot words may be passing at the present time, the game will continue – and, conceivably, emerge the better for a little blood-letting.

John Ford
West Meon

15 AUGUST 1977

CRICKET FOR SALE

SIR – Thank you for publishing Mrs Marjorie Seldon's letter (6 August). The sporting writers to the Establishment have had a long innings in showering their abuse on the men who have signed the Packer contracts. I am glad that you are giving space to another point of view.

I was brought up to believe that in this country, the proverbial home of freedom, men had the basic right of selling their talents in the most remunerative market. Apparently this is not so. Not only must professional cricketers not exercise this right but they will be deprived of their livelihood in county cricket if they do so.

The Establishment defends its attitude by alleging that Mr Packer's programme will interfere with Test match schedules. What nonsense! Packer has offered to discuss the question in order to arrive at an accommodation, but his offer has been turned down. Why?

E.K. Lumley
Kidlington

WHEN GREIG JOINED

SIR – I would suggest that Mrs Marjorie Seldon (6 August), reads your report 'Pirates to Average £20,000' (4 August) when she criticises the anti-Packer onslaught.

Also surely she is missing the point, on the Greig-joining-Packer issue – the objection is the *way* this was done without a 'by your leave' to MCC when he was captaining and playing Test cricket for England.

Lilian Halliday
Great Snoring

22 AUGUST 1977

ROYAL ASHES

SIR – It is interesting to note that the last three times the Ashes have been regained by England have been Royal occasions: the first, in 1926, was the year of The Queen's birth; the second, in 1953, was the Coronation; and the third, in 1977, is Jubilee Year.

Mrs Stella Braithwaite
Balmullo

26 AUGUST 1977

ROYAL ASHES

SIR – England also regained the Ashes here in 1893 and this was again a Royal occasion, the year of the marriage of the Duke of York to Princess Victoria Mary of Teck, later to become King George V and Queen Mary.

Marjorie Millman
London N21

23 AUGUST 1977

DRESSED FOR THE TEST

SIR – Is there any possibility of those who represent us on the international cricket field acquiring before the final Test a worthier standard of dress, decorum, dignity and deportment?

We are told that Herbert Sutcliffe, whom I often watched with the utmost pleasure during his cricket career, was a spectator at Headingley: I wonder what his impressions were as he saw men representing their country turning out in dirty flannels, grey socks (and even in two cases with 'sweat-rags'), behaving as wickets fell like excitable schoolboys rather than mature adults, and ceaselessly chewing.

Is this the standard, in cricket of all games, we want the rising generation to emulate? But perhaps permissiveness, mediocrity of standards and a low level of self-respect have already eroded the whole fabric of our national life so seriously that these subjects of distress to the older generation are now the accepted norm. *Sic transit Gloria* . . .

H.N. Duncan
Croydon

31 AUGUST 1977
DRESSED FOR THE TEST

SIR – Obviously Mr H.N. Duncan's memory does not serve him too well (23 August). While I agree that Herbert Sutcliffe was the personification of cricketing sartorial elegance, he played much of his Test cricket during a period when, I would submit, the standards of dress were far less worthy than today's.

As for 'sweat-rags', indeed it was one of Sutcliffe's England captains, D.R. Jardine, who was often to be seen sporting one (as was a post-War skipper, F.R. Brown) and it was Jardine who led the way for those who took the field in something less than the England colours, a rag-bag assortment of county caps and sweaters – and in Jardine's case the unsightly Harlequins cap on his England captain's head – seeming to be the order of the day.

Today's grey socks (which, in fact, are white with blue fleck) have for long been the 'cricketer's sock' and far from being unsightly are pleasant on the eye and – perhaps more to the point – pleasant on the foot.

No, Sir, I would contend that today's cricketer is far better dressed than his yesteryear colleague (and probably television and the media generally can take part of the credit). He takes pride in his appearance with no evidence of a crumpled shirt, with a neat sweater with England *motif* uniformly in keeping with his team-mates, an England (or MCC overseas) cap and, in the main, clean and immaculately pressed and stylish flannels.

Robert Clough-Parker
Chester

6 SEPTEMBER 1977
DRESSED FOR THE TEST

SIR – Mr Robert Clough-Parker's description of D.R. Jardine's cricketing neckwear as a 'sweat-rag' (31 August) suggests that he never saw it at close quarters. Jardine's white tie, and that of many an England Gentleman before him, bore as much resemblance to Tony Greig's knotted handkerchief as did Herbert Sutcliffe's immaculately groomed head to Willis's fuzzy mop or, for that matter, to most of the 22 haircuts on view at any Test match this season.

N. Haddock
Offwell

27 AUGUST 1977
ODD THING HAPPENED AT LORD'S

SIR – Exactly 50 years ago (Saturday, 27 August) an odd thing happened at Lord's. During the afternoon the man on the door at the Pavilion entrance told me that many members who were arriving about 12.45 that morning had asked him whether there had been rain at Lord's.

This was because Hobbs and Sandham were then batting with only five or ten runs on the board. He had replied that there had been no rain but that something else had happened.

Middlesex, winning the toss, had lost five wickets in seven consecutive deliveries – all clean bowled and with a chance of a hat-trick twice in one over – a world record (for speed) in first-class cricket.

In all the bowler had taken six wickets in 11 consecutive deliveries – a record which stood for 45 years until Pocock, another Surrey slow spin bowler, took six wickets in nine consecutive deliveries against Sussex at Eastbourne in 1972.

Many of those who played in the Lord's game have now passed on and, having gone out to grass in the country, I shall be alone with the 'glass of wine' which I always associate with Happy Memories.

Percy G.H. Fender
Broadbridge Heath

1 SEPTEMBER 1977

FENDER'S SIX WICKETS IN ELEVEN BALLS

SIR – I read with very great pleasure the letter from Mr Percy G.H. Fender, the former Surrey cricket captain (27 August). With charming modesty he omitted to say that he was the bowler who took six wickets in 11 balls during the Surrey and Middlesex match in 1927.

His analysis for the innings was seven wickets for ten runs and he took the last six wickets in eleven balls.

If I remember rightly in one over he took wickets with the first, second, fourth and fifth balls, thus missing the hat-trick twice in the same over. He took the fifth wicket with the first ball of the next over and the last wicket with the fifth ball, and six of these victims were clean bowled.

I was present at the match. Middlesex scored 54 of which Patsy Hendren made 22. After that the sun came out and Jack Hobbs and Andy Sandham came in to bat for Surrey.

Ted Beaumont
New Malden

7 SEPTEMBER 1977

FENDER AT NORTHAMPTON

SIR – Mr Percy G.H. Fender's interesting letter (27 August) reminds us how, at Lord's 50 years ago, he set a record only beaten by another Surrey bowler, Pocock, 45 years later.

What, so far as I am aware, he has never told us, is that at Northampton, less than 20 miles from Buckingham, on 26 August, 1920, four days after his 28th birthday, which I trust he celebrated with at least one glass of wine, in an innings for some reason only firstly recognised in 1936 by *Wisden*, who had previously confined their Surrey fast scoring records to the feats of F.R. Brown, J.N. Crawford and Hobbs, he reached his century in 35 minutes, a record in first-class cricket which stands to this day.

P.A. Negretti
Buckingham

12 SEPTEMBER 1977

FENDER'S WICKETS
From Major-General Sir Robert Ewbank

SIR – I apologise for out-bowling the famous Percy Fender ('Six wickets in eleven balls', 1 September). At a Fathers' Match at Springfield House Preparatory School, Horsham, a horrible little boy – without resort to 'bodyline' – dismissed seven terrified fathers with seven consecutive devastating balls!! First-class bowling even if not quite first-class cricket.

Robbie Ewbank
Rustlington

WHAT PRICE PACKER?

SIR – I am trying hard to understand the logic of the Mike Brearley statement that Packer players ought not to be considered for any future Test team.

What I would ask Mr Brearley, and indeed other cricketers not allied to the Packer side, is this: Do you not agree that whatever else, the Packer advent has injected into the game, for all to benefit, more cash?

Asking or suggesting that players of great class, now playing for Packer, should not be considered for Test matches is surely spouting double standards. Thanks very much for putting your heads on the chopping block, lads. We will accept readily the monetary awards you have gained for us. But we don't want you playing in our team.

Peter Green
Romford

METRIC CRICKET

SIR – Brigadier C.E. Lucas Phillips is worried about the length of a cricket pitch now that it must be altered to metric.

No trouble. Twenty-two yards is 20.1168 metres. Knock off the .1168, which is a mere 4.331 inches, and every fast bowler will automatically increase his speed of delivery to the batsman by 0.54684343 per cent (nearly), giving the game just that necessary fillip over the Imperial Packer Pastime.

Eric Ambrose
London NW7

12 DECEMBER 1979

RHYTHMIC CRICKET

SIR – Let us hope that Fate will arrange the following scoreline in Australia this winter: Lillee c Willey b Dilley.

Michael Kennedy
Sale

17 DECEMBER 1979

SPORTING FANCY

SIR – I, too, hope that Mr Michael Kennedy's (12 December) cricket score will come true. My favourite is 'Caught Knott, bowled Old – 0', and my favourite golf doubles pair is Grubb and Huggett.

George Gemmill
Burnley

8 AUGUST 1981

FOWLER'S MATCH

SIR – I much enjoyed Mr Michael Melford's description of Fowler's Match (5 August).

The Eton–Harrow contest at Lord's in 1910 was indeed one of the classic encounters, equal in excitement to Botham's Match. I tried to do some justice to it in my book *The Golden Age of Cricket.* But one small side-light came to my notice too late, when the book was with the printers.

Harrow in their second innings were so confident of an easy win that No. 10 in the batting order decided that he could relax in one of the tents set up at the Nursery end of the ground. He was indulging in the luxury of a cream bun when a breathless colleague burst into the tent to tell him that the Harrow wickets were falling like ninepins and that he might be needed at any moment.

He raced along the ground, stuffing the cream bun into his mouth as he ran, and reached the Pavilion just in time to buckle on his pads and get to the crease to take part in a last, but forlorn, effort to save the match for Harrow.

This story was told to me by the gallant bun-loving cricketer himself – the late Field-Marshal Lord Alexander of Tunis.

Patrick Morrah
Brighton

12 AUGUST 1981

NOT STUMPED!
From Sir Andrew Noble

SIR – I read with delight Mr Michael Melford's account (5 August) of Fowler's Match at Lord's in 1910. But he left out the last line. Jameson records in *Eton and Harrow at the Wicket*, edited by Bernard Darwin, that on the evening of the match a telegram addressed to 'Fowler's Mother London' was safely delivered to her hotel.

Those were the days!

Andrew Noble
London W8

20 AUGUST 1981

BOTHAM'S FIRST BREAK

SIR – The cartoon of the boy cricketer and the broken window in 'Peterborough' (17 August) took my memory back some 20 years to the afternoon when I, and several other members of the Mothers' Union, looked after children in the crèche at the Church Hall in Yeovil, Somerset.

Among our charges was Ian Botham, then about four years of age, who always came with a tennis ball in his pocket, with which he practised 'bowling' against the wall continuously.

In spite of all warnings from we 'umpires', the inevitable happened when he sent down a 'bouncer' and broke an electric light shade. Now, it seems, he has gone on to breaking records!

Mrs Edna M. Blackburn
Fleet

7 SEPTEMBER 1981

DAYS OF GRACE

SIR – Helen M.E. Campbell, aged 97, from Buckinghamshire, having watched the phenomenal Test series on television, has written to *The Age* of Melbourne wondering whether anyone's memory stretches back as far as hers. She recalls as a girl, spending days with her father in the ladies' stand of the Melbourne cricket ground, fortified with sandwiches and cold tea.

She recalls 'vividly' the enormous figure of W.G. Grace striding out to bat with the slight Ranji Sinhji, his silk shirt billowing in the wind, 'in, I think, 1897'. This pairing raises a difficulty since Grace last visited Australia in 1891–92 when Helen Campbell would have been about eight, whereas Ranji did not play there until 1897–98, six winters later.

Such minor confusion often happens with people many years her junior. The two separate impressions no doubt have, as it were, coalesced with time.

The Age cutting, sent by a friend, has, however, set me wondering. Does anyone living recall, for instance, Grace and C.B. Fry going out to bat at Trent Bridge in the Old Man's last Test in 1899?

Now that Ben Travers is dead, does anyone claim to have seen Jessop's epic 104 in the Oval Test of 1902?

E.W. Swanton
Sandwich

12 JUNE 1985

'BODYLINE' CANNOT BE EXCUSED

SIR – Having read your leader (6 June) about the 'Bodyline' television series I feel outraged at your attempt to whitewash this disgraceful affair.

You are not aware perhaps that Larwood, Voce and Bowes experimented with 'leg theory' in the previous summer evoking protests from Hobbs and Warner.

In his *History of Cricket*, E.W. Swanton described Larwood's bowling as 'directed at the leg stump or rather, as a rule, at an imaginary extension of the leg stump to two or three times in height'. This form of attack was described by Hobbs and Mailey as 'terrifying'.

The nadir of the tour was reached in the third Test after Woodfull was hit below the heart by a 'legitimate' ball from Larwood. Upon Woodfull's recovery, however, Jardine set the 'leg field' and instructed Larwood to bowl bodyline to the Australian captain.

Wisden described this game as 'probably the most unpleasant ever played and altogether a disgrace to cricket'.

Hobbs intimated that by the end of the tour Jardine was almost isolated and Hammond certainly declared that he would retire if 'bodyline' became a regular feature of Test and county cricket.

The few who approved of these tactics, however, must have lost some of their enthusiasm when Bob Wyatt had his jaw broken by a West Indian bowler in the following year and Hendren felt obliged to invent the first 'crash helmet'.

Perhaps this proliferation of unfair play ensured the outlawing of 'bodyline' which you do not mention.

Finally you omitted to explain that Bradman made his plea for a return to 'sanity' when the series stood at one game all, but perhaps 'on the way to a four games to one defeat' is more acceptable to you.

R. Fairclough
Prenton

13 JUNE 1985
'BODYLINE' – A CARICATURE TOO FAR

SIR – Mr R. Fairclough's comprehensive letter (12 June) has relieved me of the need to explain to those who read the sadly-mistaken leader of 6 June, headed 'We were not guilty', the true nature of bodyline bowling.

It need only be added that when MCC had digested the evidence after the team's return, and also in the light of an attempted continuation of the tactics by Nottinghamshire, they issued a specific ruling against 'direct attack' and promised the umpires full support if they found it necessary to invoke the Unfair Play law in this regard.

But may I take this opportunity of suggesting a few of the respects in which the Australian-made film disparaged Englishmen involved, rather in the manner of other films and books alleging to portray the fall of Empire?

Douglas Jardine, deluded, dauntless, trapped in an untenable situation of his own device, was far from the Nazi-ish ogre whom no team would have tolerated for a minute. Harold Larwood, shown with a snarl on his face, never hated anyone, and nor did Bill Voce – two good men led astray.

Gubby Allen never threw the ball back to his captain when asked to bowl. His attitude to Jardine is conveyed beyond argument by the letters home to his father, excerpts from which can be read in my recently-published biography.

Plum Warner was a small, bald, abstentious, soft-spoken man, not a largish, hard-drinking, finger-wagging fellow alternately blubbering and blustering.

The most ridiculous caricature of all was of Lord Harris, a universally-respected man of awesome dignity, rather than a many-chinned blimp not apparently above a spot of blackmail – this is a fictional episode with P.G.H. Fender that is contradicted by history.

Fender did not resign the Surrey captaincy to allow Jardine to proceed from that of the captaincy of England. In 1931, Jardine led England while Fender was still leading Surrey.

And poor Mr Fender! Fancy living to 92, as he has, and being portrayed as one of the more outrageous characters by P.G. Wodehouse!

E.W. Swanton
Sandwich

14 JUNE 1985

CRICKET 'NON-PERSONS'

SIR – I read with interest your leader of 6 June and subsequent letters in respect of the so-called 'bodyline' Test series of 1932–33.

The Australian Cricket Board has since that time pursued a relentless campaign to blacken the names of D.R. Jardine and Harold Larwood with some success. The English cricket establishment, while eager at the time to accept the fruits of their endeavours, have now relegated Jardine, and to a lesser extent Larwood, to the status of non-persons.

Let no one be under any illusion: had the Australians developed 'leg theory' bowling first, they would have lost no opportunity in deploying the tactic against our batsmen. The Australians have always played cricket not for its aesthetic value but with a ruthless determination to win. Lacking, however, a national depth of character, they were quick to cry foul when the same ruthlessness was used against them.

The truth of the matter is that D.R. Jardine was a gentleman, and above all a great cricketing tactician and deserves to be remembered as such.

A.J.B. Clayton
Avonwick

NO COMPLAINT

SIR – In connection with the renewed bodyline controversy, we should not forget that when Douglas Jardine was confronted himself by 'bodyline' bowling at the hands of West Indians Learie Constantine and Manny Martindale in the Test match at Old Trafford in 1933, he scored 127 without flinching. He did not complain (or is it 'whinge'?).

James D. Coldham
Woking

18 JUNE 1985

DEMON BOWLER

SIR – Mr R. Fairclough (12 June) refers to Bob Wyatt having his jaw broken by a West Indian bowler.

The bowler was Martindale, whose delivery happened to rise sharply during the final Test match in Jamaica, 1935.

I accompanied Wyatt in an ambulance to the local hospital; he never issued any complaint about the bowler. Nor did our team manager.

I am speaking from facts: since I was a member of the MCC touring team to the West Indies 1934–35.

W.E. Harbord
Harrogate

22 JUNE 1985

CRICKET 'INVASION'

SIR – The pitch invasion at the end of the first Test match was, of course, deplorable, but the supine indifference of the authorities in the face of the inevitable was even more so.

Surely, the least that could have been done as the end of the match approached, would have been an appeal over the public address system for spectators to keep off the ground until the players had left it. Had that failed then sterner measures would have been needed in future, like treating the invasion of sports grounds as trespass.

Maurice Wooller
Maidenhead

27 JUNE 1985

OPTIMIST OF THE YEAR

SIR – Prize for the optimist of the year surely should go to Mr Maurice Wooller of Maidenhead (22 June).

Did he really believe any good would have come of a broadcast appeal to spectators to keep off the ground at the end of the Headingley Test? It would have had no more effect than do such notices and adjurations as 'No bathing', 'No fishing', 'Keep Britain tidy', 'Keep off the grass', 'Keep your dog on a lead', 'Keep to the left (or right)', 'Slow, dangerous bend', 'No parking', 'Don't drink and drive'.

No. Tell people they can't do these things and must not do that, and the challenge always will be accepted.

Eric D. Todd
Manchester

27 JUNE 1985

THERE FOR THE BEER

SIR – May I comment on your leader (24 June) headed 'Time to stop louts' and J. Chamberlain's letter 'Cricket "violence"' of the same date?

Last year at Luton in the John Player League game there was a beer tent which the louts attempted to pull down and some 30 police had to be called to sort the problem out.

On Sunday last I again went to this game and what a difference. There was no beer tent, no football-style 'singing' and barracking. I saw one policeman in the ground and three directing traffic after the game.

Mrs Christine Meadows
Luton

26 JUNE 1985

THE MIGHTY FALLEN

SIR – P.G.H. Fender's death reminded me that I am probably the only woman who can claim to have bowled him out.

It was in a fathers' match at school in 1940. He hit each of my first four balls for a six, but he was clean bowled by the fifth. I have a feeling he was playing left-handed!

He was always kind and encouraging to our school team. I remember him with affection.

Mrs Jean E. Anderson
Killin

16 JULY 1985

CONTROL OF THE BALL

SIR – The recent showing on television of Fred Trueman's capture of his 300th wicket in Test cricket highlighted a difference in catching habits.

In the second Test match recently, Mike Gatting was adjudged not to have had control of the ball when attempting a catch, but Colin Cowdrey, who took the catch in Trueman's 300th wicket, made a practice of putting the ball into his pocket.

Surely this was adequate proof that he had control of the ball and many a present-day cricketer would do well to emulate this practice. Far better than throwing the ball in the air.

John Beatson
Glastonbury

20 JULY 1985
'NO-BALL' CALLS

SIR – The bowler is often warned by the umpire for running on to the line of the wicket, so too for bowling 'bouncers'.

Surely both should also be called 'no-ball'. Although the call would, probably, be too late for the batsman to take advantage, it should not be possible for him to be given 'out' from a ball which causes the bowler to be warned.

P.J. Halsey
Windsor

23 JULY 1985
BOWLERS' LUXURY

SIR – There must be many past and present long-jumpers who, like myself, cannot understand why top-class pace bowlers incur so many no-balls. In the long jump every fraction of an inch nearer to the mark helps performance and the odd no-jump is understandable. Yet, with a sensible use of markers and a disciplined run up no-jumps are kept to a minimum.

Bowlers, on the other hand, have the luxury of not needing to be close to the mark – they could be six inches or more behind with little or no effect on their performance. They have little excuse for indulging in even one no-ball. And yet they constantly do so. How very stupid it seems.

Perhaps a crack long-jumper like Lynn Davies should be called in to advise.

Brian Smith
Eastbourne

7 AUGUST 1985

THE LONG RUN

SIR – If the action of fast bowlers is studied it appears that as the ball leaves the bowler's hand he is virtually stationary.

What purpose, therefore, does the long gallop to the wicket serve?

S.W. Verey
Horley
Surrey

26 AUGUST 1985

DRESSED FOR LUNCH

SIR – Mr Michael Carey's comments on Allan Border's all-too-casual dress at the fifth Test match presentations prompts me to recall the recent Benson and Hedges Cup final at Lord's.

The Leicestershire team honoured the occasion by appearing on the balcony in their blazers, a practice they follow at Grace Road when going into the dining room for lunch – regrettably a tradition maintained by few other county cricket clubs.

> **Mrs Frances Sowden**
> Secretary
> Friends of Grace Road
> Leicester

29 AUGUST 1985

RESTRICTIONS ON BOWLER IN ONE-DAY CRICKET

SIR – The semi-finals of the NatWest Trophy competition have both emphasised what I have long believed to be an unfair feature of the present rules of one-day cricket, namely the excessive restriction on the use of any particular bowler.

An outstanding batsman can bat throughout the innings if he has the ability to do so, but an equally outstanding bowler – should one exist – is forced to cease operations once he has bowled a fifth of the scheduled number of overs.

One can, of course, see the desirability of compelling a side to include a reasonable number of bowlers rather than packing it with eight or nine batsmen, but I believe the present rule goes too far, as witness the fact that bowlers hardly ever win man-of-the-match awards in one-day games.

I suggest that the restriction on the number of overs bowled should apply only to the first three-quarters of the scheduled number of overs. For example, in a 60-over match no one would be allowed to bowl more than nine overs until 45 had been bowled, but thereafter there would be no further restrictions, and a captain would be free to make full use of whichever of his bowlers had proved most effective in the early part of the innings.

Teams would still have to include five recognised bowlers – or risk the consequences – but an outstanding bowler would be able to make just as big a contribution as an outstanding batsman, which at present he cannot.

R.F. Darling
Tynemouth

6 SEPTEMBER 1985

TACTICS IN CRICKET

SIR – Having been an avid cricket follower since the late Sixties, during which time I have seen a lot of live one-day cricket, I tend to disagree with the view of Mr R.F. Darling (29 August).

His proposed alteration to the limitation on bowlers based on the NatWest competition has a significant weakness, namely that a feature of a good captain is the tactical expertise with which he handles his bowlers within the limitations operated in all one-day games.

Within this framework a skilful captain manipulates his bowlers according to the state of the game. An opening bowler who bowls well at the start of the innings is more effective if he bowls his 12 overs in one spell, rather than return at the end of the innings for a few overs.

An exciting feature of the one-day game is that most runs tend to be scored in the last quarter of an innings. Whoever is bowling is liable to concede runs as the batting side attempts to accumulate a large total or chase a total.

Under the proposal of Mr Darling, the two most effective bowlers in the first 45 overs would be able to share the final 15 overs. However, they are likely to be as expensive as any other bowler and so the strength of Mr Darling's proposal is undermined.

Charles Day
Northampton

3 SEPTEMBER 1985

UMPIRING EXCELLENCE

SIR – The television replays in close-up and slow motion during Test matches have served at least one useful purpose. They have illustrated very clearly the tremendously high standard of umpiring at this level of the game.

A.L.H. Baylis
Steventon

5 SEPTEMBER 1985

50 EXTRAS ON THE SCORECARD

SIR – Is it surprising that England's first innings total in the final Cornhill Test included 50 extras? It used to be considered slack fielding or bowling if a side contributed more than five or six extras in an innings.

Without the 50 extras Australia would not have been obliged to follow on.

G.K. Lloyd
West Milton

29 JULY 1987

CRICKET'S BENEFITS FROM PACKER

SIR – I cannot for the life of me see what W.F. Deedes (article, 25 July) thinks the Packer affair of 1977 has to do with the present conflict between the MCC and the TCCB which is no more than a domestic squabble. The professional game of cricket in this country had been undersold for years by the muddied oafs of this world and was ripe for exploitation.

The upshot of Packer was an immediate sponsor for the county championship, the doubling of the average county player's wages and sponsored cars for the majority plus other bonuses from shirt endorsements etc. Players no longer had to work as car or insurance salesmen in the winter to make ends meet, which must be good for the game.

Ten years after Packer the game is still flourishing and the MCC and the TCCB will settle their differences as they will have to.

In ten years' time cricket will continue to prosper with, I suspect, still an enormous waiting list to join the MCC.

David Britton
Ashford

15 AUGUST 1987

SETTING AN EXAMPLE IN CRICKET

SIR – Hasib Ahsan, manager of the Pakistan touring team, described umpire David Constant as 'a disgrace' (report, 12 August). If the word disgrace is to be used at all it should be applied to the conduct of the Pakistan players on the field and their manager off the field. The latter has spent the entire tour making provocative and frequently ill-informed comments, his latest contribution being that cheating is now an essential part of the game. The same person has further had the temerity to complain of the appointment of Allan Border to captain the Rest of the World side in preference to Imran Khan!

On the field throughout the series the Pakistan cricketers have maintained a barrage of appeals – many of which have been so unrelated to the requirements of the laws of the game that they may only be construed as an attempt to pressurise and intimidate umpires; or, to be blunt, cheating.

A sad side-effect of all this is that there is always a tendency for players at lower levels of any game to emulate what they see happening at the top. My Association has been disturbed to hear of instances of similar behaviour by players in club,

village and even school games. Elsewhere in your columns
Frank Tyson refers to senior umpires who have quit the game
as a result of such lowering of standards.

We frequently receive reports of club and league umpires
giving up because they come to the conclusion that there are
better ways of spending their leisure time than offering themselves as targets for abuse and aspersions concerning their
parentage from players, who are merely reflecting the standard
of conduct and manners of their senior brethren.

Thankfully the vast majority of the cricket played in this
country still complies with the spirit of our great game. But the
cancer is spreading and can only be inflamed by examples
such as we have witnessed during the current season.

David Whiley
Chairman
The Association of Cricket Umpires
Chelmsford

2 SEPTEMBER 1987

A PITCH ADJUSTMENT TO HELP CRICKET

SIR – As we approach the close of another cricket season we
have again had the sight, not least in the televised Tests, of
umpires having to warn bowlers not to trample on the wicket
when following through. Yet there is a simple pitch adjustment
which would obviate the need for such vigilance, namely the
offsetting of wickets.

Viewed from either end, the nearer wicket should be set one
yard to the right of the centre line of the pitch; the further
wicket will of course be the same distance to the left. The
nearer bowling crease would then lie to the left of the wicket;
the popping crease would be unaffected.

The umpire would stand opposite the further wicket. Instead
of bowling 'over' or 'round' the wicket the bowler would

deliver the ball 'over' or 'round' the umpire. Hence his follow through would not interfere with the bounce of a ball bowled in the opposite direction. The mown area of the pitch would of course be wider than at present and fielders in 'silly' onside positions would be a little further from the righthanded batsman.

While on the subject of possible law revisions may I also propose a scoring change? At the moment a bowler receives no credit for a maiden over other than a round of applause and an entry in the scorebook. I suggest that for every completed maiden over two runs be deducted from the receiving batsman's score, and of course from the total, and shown in the bowling analysis. After all, if the bowler can be penalised for poor bowling (wides and no-balls) should he not be rewarded for good bowling? The possibility of a negative score might concentrate the opening batsmen's minds wonderfully!

As a tailpiece, may I further suggest that the entry Caught & Bowled on the scorecard be altered to the more logical Bowled & Caught?

H.T. Kleyn
Loughton
Essex

4 SEPTEMBER 1987
LOGIC AND CRICKET

SIR – Your correspondent H.T. Kleyn (2 September) suggests Caught & Bowled on the cricket scorecard be changed to Bowled & Caught. This is far from logical. At present, a catch is entered thus: caught Fielder bowled Bowler. A dismissal arising from the bowler catching from his own delivery would therefore logically be entered, in longhand, as caught Bowler bowled Bowler, the logical abbreviation of this being caught & bowled Bowler.

H.T. Kleyn's other revolutionary proposed alterations to the Rules are too ludicrous for comment.

There is no room for progressive thinking in cricket.

John S. Procter
London SW2

8 SEPTEMBER 1987

GIVING FIELDERS CREDIT AT CRICKET

SIR – Mr H.T. Kleyn's suggestion (2 September) that the bowler should get credit for maiden overs is ingenious but might meet with a number of objections from the authorities. I would like to suggest that the fielder responsible for a run out ought to, and very easily could, be given credit for it.

One of the best pieces of cricket in the feast of good cricket in the MCC versus World match was Harper's run out of Gooch and yet his name does not appear in Gooch's dismissal.

Of course, another fielder or the wicketkeeper can be and often is involved in the run out, but it is always the fielder who takes the major part. There can surely be no reason why his name should not be recorded and appear on the card.

Just as other statistics like 'number of catches' are noted at the end of a season, the record of numbers of 'run out' would be very interesting.

Lord Hazlerigg
Leicester

11 SEPTEMBER 1987

GIVING DUE CREDIT AT CRICKET

SIR – I fully support Lord Hazlerigg's suggestion (8 September) that fielders concerned in a run out dismissal should be named on the scoresheet. This has, in fact, occasionally been done in the past – e.g. in a Gentlemen versus Players match in 1868, and in *The Australian Cricketer* in the 1930s – but Hobbs, who is said to have thrown out from cover 15 batsmen during the 1911–12 tour of Australia, was given no credit. In recent seasons Paul Parker and Derek Randall have likewise had many direct hits – often the highlight of the day's play.

The enterprising *Wisden Cricket Monthly* has long implemented the idea of naming the fielder in Test match scoresheets. How simple it would be for others to follow this example, and how rewarding for the fielders. An entry such as 'Gooch . . . run out (Harper) . . . 117' would recall for ever an outstanding feat, and a seasonal list of the experts would be most inspiring.

Gerald Brodribb
Robertsbridge

NAMING NAMES

SIR – Lord Hazlerigg suggests that the fielder who returns the ball should be given credit for a run out.

However, not all run outs occur from brilliant fielding.

Some batsmen (it is kinder to mention no names) are well known for often being the prime cause of their partner's dismissal by a run out. Should their name be placed on the record? If so, the prospect looms of a batsman seeing his name printed several times on the scorecard for his own team's innings.

Peter Mullings
London W1

ADEQUATE REWARD

SIR – Mr H.T. Kleyn's proposal (2 September) that the wickets should be offset to prevent bowlers trampling on the wicket when following through has much good sense. But his other proposal, to reward a bowler for a maiden over by deducting two runs from the score, would be a retrograde step.

Mr Kleyn says that a good bowler should be rewarded; he *is* rewarded by taking wickets and a reward in the suggested form would have the effect of encouraging negative bowling.

A.N. Wilson
Barnet

17 JULY 1989

COMMON LAW REMEDY FOR BOUNCERS

SIR – Your admirable leading article ('A test of fair play', 15 July) on the International Cricket Council's refusal to limit the number of bouncers an over in Test cricket indicates the council's ignorance of how legal systems throughout the world can provide a remedy when sport fails to regulate itself within its own playing and administrative laws.

Violent fouling rugby and soccer players everywhere know to their cost how criminal and civil cases can always have the last word whether or not sports administrators make any effort to discipline them.

David Frith, Editor of *Wisden Cricket Monthly,* has shown what can yet happen in his book *The Fast Men.* The Sri Lanka batsman Sunil Wettimuny was taken to hospital with a badly bruised instep and ribs after he had been hit by the Australian fast bowler Jeff Thomson in the Prudential World Cup at Kennington Oval in June 1975.

Frith commented ironically after the batsman explained his injuries on arrival in hospital: 'With the timing peculiar to officers of the law, a police sergeant who had chanced to be within earshot of the conversation interjected, "Do you wish to prefer charges?"'

Since the laws of civil and criminal assault have a common

thread throughout ICC member countries, their players cannot now claim they have not been warned of the ultimate consequences if umpires and captains continue to ignore the red card principle built in to cricket's domestic legislation under Law 42 explained in your leading article.

Edward Grayson
London EC4

18 JULY 1989

REAL STORY OF BEATEN BATSMAN OF SRI LANKA

SIR – I believe I am the original source of the story of the Sri Lanka batsman Sunil Wettimuny and the policeman who wanted to charge the Australian fast bowler Jeff Thomson with G.B.H. (17 July).

It must be stressed that the diminutive and immensely brave Sunil Wettimuny at no time desired to charge Thomson. That would be completely out of character.

Wettimuny, who was hospitalised after being hit in a Prudential World Cup match at the Oval in 1975, told me the story when we met shortly afterwards at a match at Trent Bridge – we were placing bets on horses in the Ladbroke's tent. Although still heavily bandaged, he laughed loudly and joked about the London copper who thought Sunil had been attacked by a thug in the street rather than one on the greensward.

Sunil told me he had 'never thought it possible that a human being could bowl so fast'. It was not this but the foul language used on the field by both Thomson and Dennis Lillee to which he objected.

Law 46, Note 4 (IV) covers persistent bowling of short-pitched balls. Cricket does not need to call in the law, merely follow its own Laws. There should also be a law regarding abusive language on the field, which language, unfortunately, many of our modern 'sports scribes' find amusing.

Stanley Reynolds
London EC1

16 JULY 1990

SIR – One wonders whether the large number of 'no-balls' bowled in present-day cricket would be greatly reduced if they were severely punished, as they used to be.

Immediately an umpire called 'no-ball' batsmen such as Hobbs and Hammond would take a mighty wild swipe at it. Knowing they could not be given out bowled, caught or stumped, they reacted quickly, often scoring four and sometimes six runs. On the call of 'no-ball' today batsmen just raise their bats and let the ball go by.

L. Myhill
Kirkcudbright

6 AUGUST 1990

SIR – Can anyone explain why none of our Test cricketers uses a handkerchief when mopping his brow? They use collars and wrist-bands, but never a handkerchief. Can I ask their wives, girlfriends and mothers to keep them supplied with handkerchiefs?

J.M. Carter
Guildford

20 DECEMBER 1991

ARLOTT'S DELIVERY

SIR – The death of John Arlott (obituary, 16 December) will be a heavy blow to all cricket lovers, because he enriched our lives for nearly 40 years.

My favourite of so many rich items with which he regaled us goes back to a 1947 Test match when K.G. Viljeon had driven the ball out to deep extra cover. John said: 'And Doug Wright's running after it as only Doug can run: variety in every stride'. All who remember the great D.V.P. Wright's 'hop, skip and jump' run-up to the wicket will see the picture immediately. Of course, with John's deliberation and his lovely accent it sounded much better – variety in every syllable.

A.D. Mills
Totnes

9 JUNE 1993

HANDING OUT BLAME FOR CAD CALLS

SIR – As Peter Deeley (article, 8 June) points out, Graham Gooch is only the fifth Test batsman to have been given out 'handled ball'. It is one of the curiosities of the game that the first, W.R. Endean of South Africa, who caught a ball that had spun off his pad as it was dropping towards his stumps at Cape Town in the second Test against England in the 1956–57 series, had also been involved in another unusual dismissal a few years earlier.

On that occasion, at the Oval in 1951, Endean was the wicket-keeper when a ball popped up off Len Hutton's glove as the Yorkshireman attempted a sweep. As Endean lunged forward for a catch, Hutton flicked the ball away with the back of his bat and was given out for 'obstruction'.

In most of these instances – including the Gooch dismissal – it seems fair to presume that the actions of the batsmen were 'instinctive' and not deserving of censure. In some, the motives of the fielders in appealing against the batsman have been more suspect; the wretched Andrew Hilditch of Australia, batting against Pakistan, was, I believe, merely handing the ball back to the bowler, Sarfraz Nawaz.

In unprofessional circles, it is still regarded as polite for the bowler to warn the non-striking batsman who is backing up too enthusiastically before interrupting one's run-up to break the stumps at the bowler's end. Outrage was expressed at one Harrow versus Winchester game in the late 1950s when no warning was given. The cad in question, as far as I can recall, was not, as one might have surmised, a caddish Harrovian, but a member of the institution boasting the motto 'Manners Makyth Man'.

Stephen Peters
London NW8

25 JULY 1994

CRICKET FANS IRRITATED BY FOUR-DAY MATCHES

SIR – Now that the satisfying intrusion of Wimbledon, World Cup and Open golf have passed, my thoughts and interest can once again return to the cricket season.

County cricket is tremendous fun in normally tranquil surroundings, where a pint and a pie can be purchased easily between overs, amid knowledgeable, friendly folk.

Most of these folk, like me, seem irritated by the four-day game. Many matches still finish in three days, there are still run-chases on the fourth day and the record books are always open for big scores that so often deny a result, rendering that game worthless.

Let us quickly get back to the three-day games, where spectators saw more matches per season and were not left wondering how on earth to spend Tuesdays and Wednesdays for 20 weeks. These two days are very popular for watching cricket, certainly more regularly attended than Mondays or Fridays.

The whole concept of the county game has changed for the worse, with no midweek cricket, apart from some one-day matches, and no real fixtures over the May Bank holidays. It just bears no reasoning.

P. Mulford
Ruislip Manor

27 JULY 1994

ATHERTON AND THE HYPOCRITES

SIR – I believe that Michael Atherton should continue as England cricket captain. Following several days of anger, bewilderment and sadness at the furore following the dirt-in-pocket incident, I have been struck by its similarity to that of the woman taken in adultery (John, chapter VIII).

In both incidents a 'mistake' was made, and was uncontested, though Atherton's sin was in not disclosing the whole story to the match referee, Mr Peter Burge, at the first interview. This was entirely understandable. He was interviewed by Mr Burge immediately after a long and tiring day in the heat of a Lord's Test. He was no doubt flustered and somewhat uncertain as to what had or had not been seen by the cameras. He had not tampered with the ball; and there is no law which says that a cricketer may not dry his hands on dirt in his pocket.

In both cases the accusers are guilty of hypocrisy. The scribes and Pharisees of Jesus's time are now represented by the media hacks, and self-styled experts of today.

Jesus, after scribbling in the dirt (which it appears was on the ground rather than in his pocket), turns the focus back on the accusers: 'Which of you is without sin?' He then refuses to condemn the woman and urges her to 'go and sin no more'.

Atherton's disappearance from the England captaincy and even from the team would be not only a personal tragedy but a grievous loss to our cricketing ambitions – a desperate shame. He has made a mistake (in my opinion a very trivial one) and paid a heavy price financially and in public esteem.

I know Atherton to be a man of high integrity, personal charm, and inner strength. The time has come for all people of compassion and goodwill to put away the knives and rally to his support.

Reverend Andrew Wingfield Digby
Co-Director
Christians in Sport
Oxford

28 JULY 1994

WRONG ANALOGY

SIR – The Reverend Andrew Wingfield Digby's letter on the Atherton affair (27 July) cannot be left unanswered. He draws the analogy of Atherton's predicament with that of the woman taken in adultery.

Atherton is a professional, representing his country as captain; the lady shared none of these exalted achievements.

I suspect that there are many genuine cricket lovers (not media hacks and self-styled experts) who yearn to see not only the Laws, but more important the spirit, of cricket upheld and who view what occurred at Lord's with some unease.

Mr Wingfield Digby avows Atherton to be a man of high integrity and, as such, I have no doubt that he will review his position with great care.

Viscount Cobham
Stourbridge

29 JULY 1994

CLEAR CODES

SIR – The Reverend Andrew Wingfield Digby (27 July) does Michael Atherton no favours in suggesting that, when interviewed by Mr Peter Burge, 'he was no doubt flustered and unsure what the TV cameras had seen'.

If, in his own mind, Mr Atherton was convinced that he had done nothing untoward, then what the cameras had shown would have been of no consequence to him.

Although agreeing with Mr Digby that it would be a shame if Mr Atherton was lost to Test cricket, I would suggest that if he wishes to accuse anyone of hypocrisy he should turn his attention to those who have implied that the correct course of action would be for Atherton to be relieved of the captaincy, but allowed to play as a team member.

The codes of conduct must surely be the same for all – otherwise it wouldn't be cricket.

Colin Bridger
Camberley

30 JULY 1994

NO FUN AT THE WICKET ANY MORE

SIR – One of the most revealing comments on the business of what Michael Atherton was doing at Lord's with his hand in his pocket came from Denis Compton (report, 26 July). He forthrightly expressed incredulity about the whole affair.

It may be absurd to bleat on about cricket being a game when, at first-class level, it is so manifestly a decreasingly entertaining part of the entertainment industry. All the same, would it not be possible for the performers to communicate a bit more of a sense of fun?

One of Atherton's great pluses at the start of his captaincy was that he seemed a cheerful antidote to the terminally lugubrious Graham Gooch. But as he settled into the job his shoulders started to droop, he seemed to give up shaving and showed little sign of having fun.

The unrelenting commercialisation today may be the explanation. But I do not see why you should enjoy something less just because you are being paid a king's ransom for doing it.

Ian Botham, after all, must have been as well rewarded as any cricketer, but few have appeared to enjoy the game as much and, in doing so, given so much enjoyment to the rest of us. Today, we seem to have become a dour, mean-minded lot, whether in victory or defeat. One problem surely is that although many thousands of Englishmen play cricket, only a few dozen paid professionals are seriously eligible for selection to the national side.

We have not had a clergyman playing for England since David Sheppard; nor, I think, a schoolmaster since Hubert Doggart who joined the staff at Winchester in 1950, the year he played twice against the West Indies.

There must be teachers and clergymen as naturally talented as the present members of the England team, not to mention playing members of I Zingari.

Is there not some way of making the best amateurs eligible for England once again? And, if not, then of instilling some of the more cavalier instincts of the breed into the present generation?

The Grantland Rice verse about the One Great Scorer marking 'not that you won or lost – but how you played the game' does not seem to be just a housemaster's blimpishness any more.

Tim Heald
Richmond

1 AUGUST 1994

SIR – During a long and often repetitive press conference why didn't anyone say that the explanation of supposed finger drying was obviously totally inadequate. It must have been obvious to all who had seen the incident that this was clearly not the case. If Mr Atherton really believed, as he said, that he could not understand all the fuss that has been made he must be the most naïve of persons.

Andrew Saunders
North London

8 AUGUST 1994

LACK OF INTERFERENCE WITH BALL IS KEY TO PREVENTING ACRIMONY

SIR – In reference to the recent Michael Atherton affair, the controversy which surrounds ball-tampering – whether real or imagined – will surely continue to breed acrimony and sour relations between cricket-playing countries, until that practice is completely outlawed.

I subscribe entirely to the view that all interferences with the surface of the ball be forbidden. This would mean no rubbing on areas of clothing to preserve the shine, no scuffing on the ground to roughen the ball and no lifting or flattening of the seam or picking at the cover of the ball. And, of course, no 'substances', however innocuous.

The ball should be allowed to grow old gracefully and bowlers revert to plying their trade with what it offers naturally. That would happily introduce a return to the natural balance between bat and ball.

John Moran
Grantham

17 JULY 1995

SIR – Your correspondent, E. Greaves of Cheadle Hulme (10 July), re: Glamorgan versus Durham and the 'one short' called in the final over, must refer to the Laws of Cricket for the answer. Law 18, 2 (b) states: 'Although a short run shortens the succeeding one, the latter if completed shall count.' The umpire was correct.

J.L. Hubner
Isle of Wight

7 AUGUST 1995

SIR – So, those in the know call for more serious penalties on streakers who interrupt play at cricket matches.

There is no doubt that these extrovert antics make it difficult for players to concentrate, but why not crack down on that most insidious distraction, the 'Mexican Wave'. At least when a streaker struts his or her stuff, play comes to a halt. During a wave play continues, despite the extra movement and sound in the background.

I am sure that Graham Thorpe, who was out six runs short of his century while one such wave reached its crescendo, would agree with me.

Iain Martin
Hoole

21 AUGUST 1995

CRICKET BEING SHORT-CHANGED

SIR – The iniquitous bouncer requires the use of protective helmets and visors which render the batsmen unrecognisable, particularly to television viewers who cannot readily distinguish one from the other. Television commentators offer little help here. Perhaps they don't know either.

Visors restrict batsmen's vision with the result that they cannot perform at their best. Helmets cause discomfort, more obvious in hot weather, which lowers concentration and therefore peak performance.

The combined result is cricket that cannot be of the highest standard and of increasing frustration to that most important body of people – the paying or televiewing enthusiasts.

Add to this the intense distraction of screamingly brash advertising messages all over the ground and your correspondent J. Winter is undeniably justified in asking, 'What has become of our wonderful game of cricket?'

David Thomas
Buxton

28 AUGUST 1995

BASEBALL COULD HELP CRICKET

SIR – If the ICC want to limit bouncers, they cannot do it by any means that involve the umpires' discretion, as events have shown that this is exercised only in favour of the bowler.

I suggest that if a batsman is hit other than below the elbow or below the knee, extras should be credited with four runs. This would all but eliminate bouncers overnight. It is analogous to the baseball situation where if the batter is hit by a pitch, he gets a free walk to first base. If that happens at the wrong time, this could cost the pitcher's team the match. There are very few examples of batters being hit in baseball.

John Duffield
Loughton

SIR – The continuing correspondence on the subject of short-pitched fast bowling is justified by recent facial fractures to Robin Smith and Jimmy Adams. Are the powers that be waiting for a player to be killed before doing something about it?

There is a simple solution: revert to the front-foot law that used to prevail, requiring that the bowler's front foot should be behind the line at the moment of delivery.

A cricket pitch is 22 yards long. With the back-foot rule these enormous fast bowlers release the ball about 17 yards from the batsman, giving him that much less time to see it. The extra time gained from reverting to the old law would enable the better batsmen to dispense with some of their protective armour, which is a fairly recent introduction we could well do without, and which undoubtedly inhibits their view of the ball.

A. Wood
Berwick-upon-Tweed

25 SEPTEMBER 1995
GIVE STRUGGLERS AN INCENTIVE

SIR – I was interested to read in Christopher Martin-Jenkins's report of the Warwickshire versus Derbyshire championship game a suggestion that counties out of the running for the title and prize money might battle harder in late-season games if there was still something to play for.

Something must be done to avoid the trend of lowly-placed counties rolling over and dying when faced by the more motivated championship contenders.

There is surely not such a vast difference in the abilities of most of the counties as the championship table would lead one to believe. It would certainly not benefit county cricket to divide into two divisions, and the England selectors would find life even more difficult.

Your idea of prize money right down the table is excellent,

but I would go further. As the points system works, there is no reason, beyond pride, for a county unable to win a certain game to prolong it further in the second innings.

Indeed, they seem to prefer the extra time off provided by early capitulation. There must be a stronger incentive to avoid defeat.

This could be provided by a points system based on the overall result, but the points for a draw should not be numerous enough to discourage teams going flat out for victory.

A large points differential between a win, a draw and a defeat must exist. I am sure a more combative championship would result, and the bonus points system could be retained.

I have the impression that battling for a draw is completely out of fashion. It seems to have gone right through county cricket and into the England team as well. If we restore the pride to county cricket, it will surely infiltrate the international team, too.

John Crofts
Newmarket

6 OCTOBER 1995

SIR – May I add the name of another cricketer to E.W. Swanton's list of those [with] musical connections or attributes (article, 2 October).

James Cutmore, the pre-War Essex all-rounder, had a fine baritone voice and appeared in pantomime for a number of years. It can be claimed that he was the only first-class cricketer to have made a commercial record on account of his singing talent.

On a 78 r.p.m. record, bearing the Parlophone label (No. R.492), he can be heard singing *Things We Want The Most Are Hard To Get* and *Smiling Irish Eyes* released in the 1920s.

Douglas Wilkins
Worthing

15 APRIL 1996

SIR – I feel it would be quite informative if in future you printed the age of the letter-writer alongside their name. I say this because I'm sick and tired of reading letters from English cricket supporters whinging on about shaving, baseball caps, sunglasses, tucking your shirt in, not smiling enough, being aggressive and gesturing at dismissed batsmen by bowlers (Dominic Cork being regularly cited), etc.

The people who write complaining of such matters surely come from the 'Not in my day' generation of the over-fifties. When will they realise that cricket is about winning? Personally, I wouldn't care if Mike Atherton took to the field with a W.G. Grace-size beard, wearing a dressing-gown and goggles, with a fag hanging out of the corner of his mouth and swearing like a trooper, if it meant a winning England team.

D.M. Hamsworth
(Aged 29)
Brighton

22 APRIL 1996

SIR – D.M. Hamsworth, aged 29, asks when we shall realise that cricket is about winning (15 April). Some of us agree with Don Mosey, who said in his book *The Best Job in the World* that 'the man who goes to a cricket match, any match, to see one side win rather than to enjoy the game itself is, to me, always going to miss the real essence of cricket'.

Roy Butterfield
(Aged 48)
Keighley

SIR – Your correspondent, D.M. Hamsworth, has correctly pointed out that cricket is about winning. However, he would do well to note that it was way back when sportsmen dressed properly that England could boast winning teams, not only in cricket, but in football and various other sports. Probably, at the age of 29, he is too young to remember.

K.S. Knowles
(Aged 70)
Ashill

SIR – The 29-year-old, Mr Hamsworth, has hit the nail right on the head. His attitude to English cricket being 'all about winning' regardless of the spirit in which the game is played says much about modern-day cricket's malaise. What a shame that Mr Hamsworth's generation will never experience the game as it was intended to be played, even in my day.

P. Robinson
(Aged 58)
Berlin Cricket Club

SIR – I see that the future of English cricket is in good hands. On Tuesday, Hampshire scored 450 against England Under-19s with 86 extras, including nine wides and 38 no-balls.

I suppose that, like the police, umpires are no longer allowed to administer a clip around the ear to an errant youth.

Peter Thompson
Sutton

29 JULY 1996

SIR – As a member of MCC for 30 years, I am intrigued that the question of women members has risen once more.

I wonder how many women, having obtained membership, would be willing to join the scrum to obtain seats in the Pavilion for a Test, join the queues for a cup of coffee and generally be pushed and shoved – something we all enjoy as part of a Lord's Test.

To alter and inevitably enlarge the Pavilion to accommodate the women would lead to greatly increased subscriptions all round.

So who would benefit from all this? Very few members, and only some women who would derive pleasure in disrupting what is a harmless male preserve, and just because it is all-male.

Me? I have reached the age when I can no longer enjoy such a privilege, so have done the decent thing by resigning, thus allowing someone else (male) to enjoy what has given me so much pleasure.

Richard J. Piner
Kingsbridge

SIR – As a female cricket enthusiast, I would, of course, like to be able to join MCC but nevertheless regard admitting women (including me) to memberships as a great mistake. Let MCC invite eminent women cricketers to join, perhaps, but otherwise the club should be kept as a male haven – there are few enough left.

In an attempt to be politically correct, the Sports Council, among others, seem to have lost all sense of proportion. It now appears that MCC members are having difficulty maintaining their preferred way of life so they should qualify as a 'minority group' and, as such, be entitled to funding to enable them to carry on in their chosen way.

Mrs R.J. West
Henley-on-Thames

16 SEPTEMBER 1996

SIR – How would Imran Khan have felt, I wonder, if he had been told as a young man that he had been selected to play cricket for his country but would never be allowed to play in Pakistan? Sounds preposterous, I know, but this, in effect, is what he is suggesting – with boring regularity – should be the fate of international umpires.

In his column on 9 September, he says that he found the quality of the umpiring throughout the summer Test series poor and then follows this by suggesting we have two neutral umpires. Surely what is wanted is the best umpiring available in the country where the matches are being played, so does Imran think that this would mean the home team had an unfair advantage?

Sarah Alexander
Hove

28 OCTOBER 1996

SIR – You report (18 October) that Hansie Cronje, the South African cricket captain, won admiration for recalling Sourav Ganguly to the crease after he had been run out while crashing into the bowler, Fanie de Villiers.

How I wish that I could imagine an England captain doing this during a Test match. It is nice to know that the cavalier spirit still exists in cricket, albeit outside of these shores.

Colin Murray
Aylesford

3 DECEMBER 1996

ON THE LEVEL

SIR – I may be naïve, but can anyone tell me why a 'level playing field' should have become a metaphor for fairness?

In what games are there 'unlevel playing fields' that give an advantage to one side rather than the other? In rugby, football, baseball, tennis and ice hockey, individuals or teams always change ends during a match to ensure that no one is disadvantaged by unlevel conditions.

In cricket an unlevel playing field (the condition of the wicket) and how to manipulate it are part of the tactics. Isn't it time this meaningless metaphor was relegated into the limbo of forgotten clichés?

Milton Shulman
London SW1

11 DECEMBER 1996

PITCH THEM IN

SIR – Watching the Sky advertisement for its coverage of the England winter cricket series, I was wondering whether there is a collective name for a group of unsuccessful captains – Atherton, Gower, Botham and Willis, for example?

Perhaps 'collapstains'?

Michael Brown
Melksham

12 DECEMBER 1996
HOWZAT?

SIR – Further to Michael Brown's collective name for a group of unsuccessful England cricket captains (11 December), perhaps they should be known as caught-marshals.

Malcolm Cornberg
Yeovilton

13 DECEMBER 1996
PLAYED OUT?

SIR – A collective noun for England cricket captains (11 December): 'Loss-leaders'?

Leslie Fraser-Mitchell
Swaffham

6 JANUARY 1997

SIR – Martin Johnson commented on the Duckworth/Lewis method that was used for recalculating the target in the second one-day international in Harare. He referred to it as 'so indecipherable that the Admiralty might be interested in it for a new code'.

Implementation of the method requires a table of figures that provides the information required: in this case, that with 42 overs to face and all ten wickets in hand, a team would be expected on average to make 92.5 per cent of the score they would attain in the full 50 overs, this figure being based on the experience of several hundred one-day international matches. All that needed to be calculated was 92.5 per cent of 200, which gave 185 as the revised target.

With the new method, England's task of scoring 185 in 42 overs was just as challenging as scoring 200 in 50.

John Carr
Cricket Operations Manager
English Cricket Board
London

4 MAY 1997

SATURDAY SLIP-UP

SIR – So Brian Downing, chairman of the ECB's marketing advisory committee, is concerned that cricket membership has remained static since 1980 and that the membership age is rising ever further.

Perhaps Mr Downing should discuss this with whoever made the ludicrous decision that county championship matches are to conclude on a Saturday this season. From recent experience, while there may be the occasional exciting last day, many of the matches will already be over or so near to conclusion that hardly anyone will attend. This is no way to attract new members who are younger and still working during the week.

A.J. Gillingwater
Chingford

27 JULY 1997

TWENTIES THROWBACK

SIR – What I have to say seems so obvious that it is surprising nothing has been done about it before now.

Batsmen, quite rightly, usually receive the benefit of the doubt when the umpire's decision is required, but why should they receive it for deliberately and repeatedly using their pads, with or without the camouflage, to play at balls pitched outside the off-stump? There is no need to play at such a delivery if a batsman thinks it is going to miss the wicket. Therefore by using his pads there must be some doubt in his mind, for which a bat has been provided, but he might be caught, so he employs the safer option.

Well, it would not be the safer option if batsmen could be given out for such tactics, and I am reminded of the lbw rule used by children in the backstreet in the 1920s. If you were hit on the legs three times you were out, which may not find favour at Headquarters but at least the batsman would know where he stood.

The present lbw law would not need amending, but umpires should be able to give batsmen out, after one warning, 'deliberate obstruction', instead of the present alternative of repeated 'not outs', even if the ball would have missed the wicket.

K.H. Bradley
Kendal

21 JULY 1997

SIR – Peter Cotterall (14 July), referring to the Blewett–Hussain catch controversy, implies that the fielder is always in a position to confirm whether a catch has carried. This is frequently not the case. As a study of various photographs will show, most fielders involuntarily close their eyes a split-second before the ball impacts with their hands.

This is particularly noticeable when they are diving forward, as Hussain was in the instance in question. Thus, as I know from experience, the fielder must go on the feeling of the ball as it hits the hands. Since a half-volley and a fair catch frequently feel identical, the 'catcher' is sometimes in a poor position to judge the legitimacy of the appeal.

On a number of occasions I have initially claimed a catch only to be told by my fellow fielders that the ball has not carried. I therefore feel that it is unfair of Mr Cotterall to question Hussain's honesty. Under these circumstances a fielder has to rely on the integrity of his team-mates and the judgment of the umpires.

N. Devereux
Woodford Green

11 SEPTEMBER 1997
COUNTY FEARS

SIR – The proposed split of the county cricket championship into two divisions (5 September) will certainly damage some of our much-loved clubs so that those who get stuck 'below the line' will face life-threatening repercussions.

The agent of a star overseas cricketer is unlikely to commit his client to second division status. Only a 'premier' player will attract the major commercial spin-off, and the England selectors will place more importance on performance in the first division than in the second.

Should a county club lose its better players to the top division then it is likely to remain in the lower pool, see its membership fall and its sponsors either turn away or negotiate reduced financial packages. Some long-established counties may shrink, and even sink.

Tony Lewis
Llantrisant

23 FEBRUARY 1998

SIR – Could it be that the failings of our cricketers over the past few years can be linked in any way to the growing fashion in the team for sporting ridiculous-looking sunglasses? Is it possible that a ban on the wearing of such glasses may, in fact, contribute to an improvement in the team's performance?

If nothing else, it may make it easier for the players to find their razors and have a shave.

Dominic Johnson
Horsham

28 FEBRUARY 1998
LADIES' MAN

SIR – In its determination to keep the ladies out of the Long Room at Lord's (report, 25 February), MCC seems to have forgotten an incident which it might care to ponder.

During A.E.R. Gilligan's 1927 tour of India, a women's team inflicted the only defeat on the club at Delhi when P.T. Eckersley, remembered today as a plucky batsman and high-class close-in catcher, turned out for the women dressed for the part. Eckersley was none the worse for the experience, since he went on to captain Lancashire and became a Unionist MP. He was killed in 1940 in a flying accident while with the Fleet Air Arm.

I might add that, during the same tour, the future England captain R.E.S. Wyatt rode round the pitch on a motorcycle during one interval wearing a woman's hat.

Gerald Hill
London EC2

16 MARCH 1998

SIR – Another anecdote about Brigadier 'Birdie' Smith (obituary, 10 March), which he told me himself: After the loss of his arm meant he could no longer play cricket, he umpired Service games. When a batsman hit a six (signal, two arms raised above the head), an Australian voice cried: 'How're you going to signal that one, Brig?'

Birdie responded by raising his one arm, and two fingers, to the sky.

Bernard Clark
Sidmouth

4 MAY 1998

SIR – Cricket's logic continues to defy me. As a Kent supporter I was horrified to discover probably our most attractive championship match – against Middlesex – buried in wind and rain at Canterbury in mid-April. A bit like Arsenal playing Manchester United on a Tuesday morning in July.

Kent then followed the rain to Cardiff. They scored more runs than Glamorgan (308 to 275), took only two fewer wickets and came within two wickets of winning yet still attracted only four bonus points to Glamorgan's seven.

I think I'll stick to a sport that awards three points for a win, one for a draw. I can understand that.

Brian Moore
ITV
London

29 JUNE 1998

SIR – I remained loyal to Fearnley bats for 15 years and, contrary to what you said (6 June), was not 'lured away' by Slazenger for 'improved financial terms'.

When my contract came up for renewal, Fearnley sought a substantial reduction in my remuneration which I could not accept. My offer to meet them half way was rejected but, happily, I was able to sign up on those reduced terms with Slazenger.

Graeme Hick
Worcester

27 JULY 1998

SIR – Reading E.W. Swanton's excellent article on W.G. Grace reminds me of tales my uncle, A.J.L. Hill of Hampshire, The Gentlemen and England, told me: W.G. was not above using some low cunning to achieve his ends. In one county match an opposing bat was making a huge score. W.G. suddenly pointed at the sun and said to him: 'Could you hit that one?' Then he called to his bowler, 'put it down quick', and the batsman, still dazzled, was bowled.

R.K. Page
County Wicklow

14 AUGUST 1998
BAN REPLAYS

SIR – Cricket umpires are not infallible (12 August); they make a judgment based on the evidence available. All of us, including lawyers, doctors and policemen, are capable of making poor judgments from time to time.

I do not believe that technology, mooted by some self-styled media cricket experts, would do anything other than harm the game. Neither the crowd nor media commentators are in any position to make a better decision than the umpire. Television replays and the dreary expert analyses of an umpire's decision serve only to aggravate rather than allow one to enjoy the game. The solution is simple. Ban all TV replays.

John Rothwell
Bray

15 AUGUST 1998

UMPIRE'S CALL

SIR – As a television recording engineer I would like to point out that the real problem with cricket umpires and replays (14 August) is the television frame rate (pictures per second).

There are only 25fps, which is far too slow for cricket balls flashing about at 80 m.p.h. plus.

But the exposure time is about the same as that of the old 'Box Brownie' camera. When people are viewing the tape frame for frame – which includes an equal 'blank period' between each of the frames – an incident in a match has to be fairly obvious for them to be sure what happened.

The umpire's continuous vision is often the most reliable.

Bernard Mattimore
Blewbury

2 NOVEMBER 1998

SOLD FOR POT OF GOLD

SIR – Jim Swanton's words (26 October) made welcome reading for true devotees of county cricket. Many will feel their county officials have sold them off for a pot of gold – and trouble is brewing in the shires.

It has taken a long time for the truth to dawn that there is little relationship between the county cricket programme and the success of the England team. The needless tampering has caused much damage to county cricket.

My hope now is that the first-class counties will be financed to become 18 centres of excellence – starting in the schools – and the county programme will be reviewed with full consideration for its past strengths.

In my view these include: the greater entertainment and certainty of three-day cricket; true seven-day festivals around the country; and the immediate return of the early-season 50-over competition with its divisions and high-summer final (played in white clothing).

Forget meaningless regional cricket played in a vacuum – let us have a highly competitive county programme to enthuse the traditionalists again but which has a real chance of attracting more young people. It is a time to look backwards and forwards.

Dennis J. Fowle
Life Member
Kent County Cricket Club

23 NOVEMBER 1998

SIR – I have just watched a television interview with Sir Donald Bradman in which he said there was no sledging at all in his Test career. Last week, in a similar TV interview, Colin Cowdrey said exactly the same. Both said that they and their fellow captains would not have allowed it.

Their Test careers span cricket from the Twenties to the Seventies, so when and how did this obnoxious practice start? Surely the umpires should be instructed to put an end to it and receive all support from above in doing so?

R.E. Groves
President
Shropshire Cricket Association

14 DECEMBER 1998
BUTTING IN

SIR – By using goats to mow the outfield (Peterborough, 11 December), Builth Wells Cricket Club runs the risk of the traditional grass stains on white flannels giving way to something more sinister. Perhaps the tendency to multi-coloured and dark clothing for the game might now make sense to the traditionalists.

Peter Middleton
Gawsworth
Cheshire

7 JANUARY 1999
MORE IMPORTANT

SIR – I notice that David Lloyd, the England cricket coach, is reported as saying: 'I want us to be more aggressive. I want us to be more in the face and I want us to hustle and have more intensity.'

Might I suggest, as an alternative, he finds a team who holds its catches, includes batsmen who score runs consistently and possesses a spin bowler who actually turns the ball?

Peter Baker
Osterley

26 JANUARY 1999
BEECH TREE RULES

SIR – Further to Roderick Staples's letter concerning the lime tree at Canterbury cricket ground (25 January), I remember a specimen copper beech tree at Welton cricket club, near Daventry.

During the Fifties, it was a 'local rule' that if a cricket ball was hit into the tree, the batsman could be dismissed if a fielder caught the ball one-handed.

This was not always easy as the ball tended to ricochet from branch to branch on its way down and its emergence from the boughs could not be predicted until the last moment. Sometimes the ball would fall to the ground after a few seconds and elude more than one fieldsman, and it was often the chance for the batsman to turn one run into two as the ball slowly came down.

Peter Kemp
Epsom

12 FEBRUARY 1999

IN THE BOOK

SIR – You say that Richard Stokes's feat of witnessing both cases of bowlers taking all ten wickets in a Test 'will never appear in *Wisden*' (report, 10 February). I can assure you that it will. It is probably more impressive than the bowling.

Matthew Engel
Editor
Wisden Cricketers' Almanack
Newton St Margarets

22 FEBRUARY 1999

SIR – It was bound to come – modern technology has overtaken cricket. A report in *The Daily Telegraph* (17 February) said that first-class umpires were to have computer-simulated training to help them make future decisions correctly, particularly in relation to leg before wicket, where most mistakes are said to occur. When I played, just before and just after the War, we used to give the umpire a white stick!

Leslie Fraser-Mitchell
Swaffham

3 MAY 1999

CAUGHT OUT

SIR – One cannot help wondering whether a brief news item on 30 April might have some bearing on England's lack of success in Test matches. No fewer than four – yes, four – Kent county cricketers divulged their bank-card PIN numbers over the telephone to a thief who had stolen their cards after he said he was a policeman, had caught the thief and needed to confirm the victims' identities. Footballers, perhaps. But cricketers?

Stan Druitt
Peterborough

7 JUNE 1999

SIR – If it is thought that English cricket is in the middle of a slump at the moment, we should spare a thought for its future. Corridor and dormitory cricket have just been banned at my school and if this crucial grass-roots level of the sport ceases to exist, many future stars may never develop in the way they should.

Joel Chase
Monkton Combe School
Monkton Combe

14 JUNE 1999

SIR – I am writing with regard to your article of 5 June concerning the Leicestershire versus Glamorgan county championship match, the headline of which made reference to Michael Kasprowicz as a 'pie thrower'.

The Glamorgan and the Leicestershire players and myself thought the article very unjust to Michael.

He has bowled very well for us and we are delighted with his contribution, both on and off the field. Unfortunately, since the headline appeared, several opposition supporters have, in their verbal abuse of him, latched on to the 'pie thrower' description.

We believe that *The Daily Telegraph* always gives a good and fair description of the game, but in this case you have erred.

Jack Birkenshaw
Cricket Manager
Leicestershire County Cricket Club

5 JULY 1999

SIR – County cricket has lost its magic, at least the four-day game has. The robot players in their helmets and visors, looking like medieval warriors, have made the game a grim business, with each batsman losing his individuality.

Then there is the deadly slowness of the cricket, with the side batting first, having worn down the bowlers, content to bore the spectators by prolonging their innings until tea on the second day at least.

A new law should be introduced, stating that each side's first innings last for one day only. A few years ago, during the three-day match era, there was a limit of 100 overs for the team batting first and this usually meant that the other side would be batting before close of play. Much more interesting for the spectators.

Robert Day
Canterbury

30 AUGUST 1999

SIR – Following the recent articles by Michael Henderson on Sir Neville Cardus and Ted Dexter on cricket techniques, you might find the following quotation from Sir Neville in 1938 apposite.

'It is impossible to judge from performances in county cricket whether any player – save the obviously great, such as Hammond – will be any good in a Test match. County cricket nowadays does not challenge either character or a comprehensive technique.'

Is there anything new under the sun?

Paul Hughes
Abersoch

17 FEBRUARY 2000

LEVELLING PITCH

SIR – European history might have evolved in quite different fashion had the French taken up cricket a couple of hundred years ago (16 February).

In his *English Social History*, G.M. Trevelyan points out how English village cricket has always cut across social boundaries, with squire and blacksmith playing side by side.

He concludes: 'If the French noblesse had been capable of playing cricket with their peasants, their chateaux would never have been burnt.'

June Gould
London W5

LET THEM PLAY CRICKET

SIR – If only the French had behaved themselves better in 1789, they might not have had to wait until now to discover the civilising joys of cricket (21 February).

According to an article in *The Daily Telegraph* that appeared on 1 April, 1989, the British government was planning to send a cricket team to Paris just before the outbreak of revolution. The plan was apparently conceived by our ambassador to the court of Versailles, the Duke of Dorset, one of the drafters of the original laws of MCC, as a goodwill gesture that might stave off unrest.

The XI was to include the Earl of Tankerville, a notorious rake, and nine other gentlemen and players, most of them members of Chertsey Cricket Club. The 11th man was to be none other than Dorset himself.

Alas, it was not to be. The gallant volunteers reached Dover harbour on 10 August, 1789, only to be met by the horror-stricken figure of their 11th man, who had resigned his ambassadorship and was returning to London with ghastly tales of mob violence in Paris.

Had revolution not broken out, England might be facing France rather than Australia at Lord's; conversely, had the cricketers got their act together sooner, France might still have a Bourbon king.

The day after the *Telegraph* article appeared, it was hailed by the *Mail on Sunday* as the best April Fool's spoof in the press. But the honour was undeserved: every word was true.

Adam Swinnerton
Wokingham

25 APRIL 2000

BLACK MARQUE

SIR – Your report of 19 April says that Hampshire County Cricket Club have provided their new Australian bowler, Shane Warne, and his wife with a pair of BMWs. It would have been much nicer to read that they had been provided with a pair of Rover 75s.

A.R.G. Burgess
Waltham Cross

12 JUNE 2000

COMPTON HELPED LIGHTEN DARK DAYS

SIR – Compton a cavalier batsman of a golden age? Surely this observation by Michael Henderson (2 June) is the product of either defective memory or rosy-hued sentimentalism.

Were not the post-War years – the core of the great Compton's Test career – largely depressing ones for English cricket, as it bravely and often vainly struggled for rehabilitation after domestic cricket's six-year stoppage? Thrashed in Australia (1946), 52 all out at the Oval (1948) and outclassed throughout that summer, they were forced to rush out Hutton to the Caribbean to bolster an ailing side (1947). England had to field teams in which only Compton himself, Hutton, Bedser and Evans could be called truly world class, in which there was no real fast bowler until Trueman in 1953, and in which the journeymen of county cricket found a ready place because there was nobody else.

The bulk of Compton's career was certainly played in a 'golden age' of Australian cricket (Bradman, Lindwall, Miller, Morris, Harvey *et al*) but any gold relating to the post-War domestic game was of a much duller hue.

If, however, Mr Henderson is referring to how the game was

played, manners on and off the field, the knowledgeable crowds who packed the grounds, the absence of sledging, pyjamas, the ghastly reverse paddle, the one-day slog and barmy armies, I shall be the first to subscribe to his 'golden age'.

Clive Tregarthen Mumford
St Mary's
Scilly

17 JULY 2000

SAFETY OF OUR CHILDREN MUST BE PARAMOUNT

SIR – I was surprised and dismayed at Donald Trelford's article (11 July) about helmets for junior cricketers.

I would agree that the England and Wales Cricket Board directive has been hastily implemented and ill thought-out with regards to supply and cost etc, but the overriding concern for the safety of our children playing potentially dangerous sports must be paramount.

My son, Peter, is a Lancashire Under-15s triallist and an England triallist at hockey, with a keen eye and excellent reactions. They weren't good enough to save him from a medium-pace accidental beamer during a school match. The ball smashed his brace and broke his jaw. He was lucky that the brace prevented the broken jaw from displacing.

Mr Trelford's casual attitude to such serious incidents is a throwback to the stiff upper lip, grin-and-bear-it attitude of years gone by. He also inferred that such incidents are few and far between, yet I would suggest that all cricketers can tell stories of team-mates or opponents having teeth removed or bones broken by top edges.

It would seem that Mr Trelford expects the best players to take protective measures, whilst the poorest and least experienced (i.e. eight-year-olds) should be discounted from such measures. A few thousand helmets would be comparatively cheap expense for the ECB and counties if they place great value in developing our youth.

Neil Flanagan
Bolton

7 AUGUST 2000

SPECTATORS DESERVE BEST

SIR – On Channel 4's *Cricket Roadshow* (29 July) I watched with some dismay a group of cricketers debating the ECB's decision to pull certain international players out of the county game in advance of Test matches and tours.

It is understandable that the cricketers think it is not a bad idea – the counties get financial compensation, the selected players get a paid holiday and some borderline county cricketers get an extra game or two. But what about the spectators, the county cricket club members? We want to see our county do well, and we want to see the star performers.

When I go to watch cricket at Taunton, I want to see Caddick and Trescothick perform. If Yorkshire are the visitors I want to see Gough and White in action. That is half the pleasure of cricket-watching – seeing the pike gobble up the minnows.

Michael Barber
Somerset

8 AUGUST 2000

WELSH BALLS

SIR – Usk's example of 'sportsmanship' in the Wadworth 6X National Village Cricket Championship reminds me of my own first experience of cricket in the principality when, evacuated to Wales, my Kent school played its first cricket match against a Welsh school.

Our captain bowled out the Welsh captain with the first ball. 'Not out,' cried the Welsh. 'First ball is always a trial ball . . .' Being a sportsman, our captain accepted the apparent Welsh custom.

Roy Baker
St Albans

13 NOVEMBER 2000

SIR – I was astonished to read about the investigations of so-called match-fixing in county cricket. This is as shambolic as it is ridiculous. We are all able to make pretty sound judgments to fit any occasion with the benefit of hindsight, especially being aware of the outcome of a particular cricket match.

No investigation can examine realistically the atmosphere surrounding the game when a declaration is made. It may result in the outcome being extremely tight and not necessarily bring the result expected. I am confident that any more tampering or investigations will result in captains not taking a chance, and cricket will be the loser.

Martin Wraith
Cottingley

27 FEBRUARY 2001
BRADMAN'S FINEST

SIR – There cannot be many who, like myself, were present at Lord's in 1930 when Don Bradman made most of the 254 runs in what he regarded as his finest innings. He scored at a great pace, never lifting the ball off the ground but placing it wide of the fieldsmen.

'Gubby' Allen, the England captain who had also been my

cricket captain at Eton, told me afterwards that Bradman had sat for three hours in the pavilion with his pads on waiting to go in. What was extraordinary was that, in his first ball, he was still confident enough to go halfway down the wicket to stroke the slow left-handed bowler J.C. White for a long single.

Earl of Longford
London SW1

28 FEBRUARY 2001
CRICKETING DISCIPLINE

SIR – When I interviewed Donald Bradman in Melbourne at the end of his career in 1948, he ascribed his success to 'concentration', and being the captain at the bridge. 'You will have noticed,' he said, 'I am alone here in the Oriental Hotel. The team is across the road at the Occidental. Discipline is essential in a Test XI.' A lesson for today?

Edward Bishop
St Leonards
East Sussex

5 MARCH 2001

SIR – In 1948 at the age of 15, I got the tram to the Oval to see Surrey play Australia. It was Don Bradman's last tour and I hoped fervently the great man would play. He did and the Australians batted. The Don came in around midday. At about 3.30, he was out after scoring an effortless hundred-plus. He was given a standing ovation back to the pavilion, the next batsman came in and play resumed.

After about ten minutes, there was a strange rattling sound around the ground. It soon dawned on me that it was the clicking of various turnstiles. People were leaving in droves.

They had seen Bradman bat and nothing more the tourists could do would match that.

W. George Preston
Locks Heath

SIR – In Martin Johnson's article (27 February) mention is made of Sir Donald Bradman's rare flashes of humour, which was greater than it appears.

In the early Seventies I was in a lift in the Cricketers' Club of New South Wales in Sydney when Bradman entered on a day when newspapers had reported that he was unwell.

Someone inquired after his health and Sir Donald replied as quick as a flash: 'I've never felt better and all those stories in the papers are based on rumours spread about by my florist and undertaker.'

A private man with a typical dry Australian sense of humour.

David Andrews
Tenterden

12 MARCH 2001

UMPIRES CAUGHT BY CON MEN

SIR – May I contribute to the debate on umpiring standards. It seems to me that the modern Test umpire has a thankless task. He has to stand for five days arbitrating between two sets of con men: batsmen do not walk when they are clearly out, and bowlers and wicketkeepers make ludicrous appeals.

Basically the modern player cheats. The more successful sides cheat more successfully. This seems to be what today's players want. They euphemistically call it tough or hard cricket. That is fine, but they should not whinge when the other finest players in Europe. He is neither stupid nor dishonest, as the article infers, but quite capable, as are many of his colleagues, of playing an increasingly demanding game with passion and decency.

Experienced journalists should avoid making generalisations, and Mr Parkinson's assertion – that all footballers are incapable of conducting themselves responsibly – is as tiresome as the anecdotes about his Barnsley heroes.

M.W.G. Short
Pickering

26 MAY 2001

PRINCIPLE OF 'WHITES'

SIR – In Charles Randall's report about the Australians wanting to wear coloured clothing in a first-class match (25 May), John Carr of the English Cricket Board says: 'It's entirely logistics. There's no big principle happening here.'

If there isn't a 'big principle' happening here, there should be. Over recent years, cricket has already lost far too much of what had made it the greatest game, whether from dishonour, corruption, pyjamas, on-the-pitch advertising or any number of other unwelcome intrusions. Surely it is not too much to ask for the most basic 'dignity' of cricket to be upheld by the retention of whites for the 'real' game?

If it really is 'entirely logistics', this raises the question of whether the Australians' baggage master has ever heard of courier companies. It should not be that difficult to arrange for excess clothing to be sent back to Lord's or wherever for the duration of the post-Worcester pyjama-tour, to be collected when cricket proper resumes a month later.

John Fingleton
London W1

gave the name of my synagogue. There was no third question. English attitudes have not changed much in 40 years.

Stuart Williamson
London NW4

18 JANUARY 2002
PREGNANT PAUSE

SIR – Reading of the England cricketer Ashley Giles worrying about leaving his pregnant wife to go on tour reminded me of the time in 1940 when I and thousands of other pregnant wives were left alone to cope while our husbands were on war duty.

After our daughter was born my husband inquired of his CO whether he could have 48 hours' leave to come and see me. His reply was: 'Is it necessary as I see from the telegram that mother and baby are doing well?' I am glad to report that he did get leave and we were eventually able to enjoy 62 years of marriage. Tell Mrs Giles not to worry – absence makes the heart grow fonder.

Joan Webb
Needham Market

22 MARCH 2002
KEEP CHEWING

SIR – The University of Northumbria's research into chewing gum as an aid to concentration (report, 14 March) is welcome.

The university may be inclined to broaden its research into other practical uses. It is known, for instance, that RAF plane crews got home safely by sealing oil and petrol lines with chewing gum residue. The product is also used as a temporary stop to leaking radiators and punctures, especially in bicycles.

Though chewing gum helped my own concentration when I was managing director of the Wrigley Company, I found it impossible to chew and dictate at the same time. So, in order to help the company grow, I chewed gum to meditate and plan growth strategy.

The dental profession is pro-gum chewing as an aid to healthy teeth. And it is likely that the England cricket team's current improvement – bowling and batting – owes some of its success to better, sustained concentration, due to chewing gum.

Frank Hoppe
Week St Mary

20 APRIL 2002
UNFAVOURABLE ODDS

SIR – The official start of the cricket season yesterday reminded me that there are approximately 40 million alternatives (11 factorial for the mathematically minded) for a captain to list his team's batting order.

Let us hope that at least one combination can prove successful.

William Haly
London SW6

1 MAY 2002
HEALTH RISK

SIR – There is almost certainly a sound basis for Tony Moore's suggestion that the excitement caused by the improved showing of the England cricket team in 2001 was responsible for the 66 per cent increase in the average annual death rate of members of MCC (29 April).

This comes as no surprise to those of us who have always understood that people who follow cricket do so because they find activities such as bowls, marbles and trainspotting too exhilarating.

Colonel David Whitaker
Chawton

12 JULY 2002
LACK OF BATTING

SIR – The first appearance of the first-class averages reveals the daftness of the present arrangements that are inhibiting our players. In the first week of July the highest number of innings by any batsman was 15. Michael Vaughan, one of our best, has been to the wicket only eight times in eleven weeks. Are we, seriously, to believe that this is too much cricket?

'A thousand in May' used to be a target; now it seems that a thousand in the season will do. Talk about money for old rope!

Phillip Fowler
York

23 AUGUST 2002
TRUEMAN BEST

SIR – Martin Johnson's assertion that Fred Trueman and his fellow fast bowlers were fitter than the present pacemen (9 August) brought disdain from Mr R. Jones (16 August).

Trueman played for Yorkshire from 1949 to 1968. Apart from the Gillette Cup, which began in 1963, he played little one-day cricket – certainly not international games, which began in 1971. Six John Player League matches for Derbyshire in 1972 ended Fred's career.

Five times, in 1954, 1957, 1963, 1964 and 1966, he bowled more than 800 overs in an English season. In 1955 he bowled 996 overs; 1959: 1,077 plus 342 winter tour overs; 1960: 1,068 plus 114; 1961: 1,180; 1962: 1,141 plus 121.

Having, in 1962, bowled 1,141 overs and taken 153 wickets, on the boat journeying to Australia Trueman declined to join Gordon Pirie's running group – a decision justified when, in that tour, he took 55 wickets.

Of course, the modern one-day game has resulted in vastly improved, acrobatic fielding. Modern advancements in the physical sciences, training methods and diet should make the modern player the fittest.

However, dressing-rooms resemble hospital casualty wards. Today, the 12th, 13th and 14th man is as suntanned as the rest of the team.

Certainly, neither Trueman nor Brian Statham, as fleet-footed and sure-armed as any of today's boundary fielders, would hurl himself around in a vain attempt to save an odd run and risk injury. Indeed, Trueman spent much of his time fielding at short leg, where many of his 439 catches were taken.

Even the lack of helmets, padding and other equipment, now deemed essential for batting, did not deter the cricketer of old. Leather ankle-height boots proved more substantial than modern lightweight shoes.

Maybe Trueman's side-on bowling action, which many experts described as almost perfect, had something to do with his longevity.

The latest find, Simon Jones, has an action no self-respecting schoolteacher would allow an 11-year-old to develop.

The modern thoroughbred or the old-fashioned, reliable workhorse? Give me the durable Bedsers, Stathams and True-mans every time.

Robert Ian Smith
Farnham Royal

16 AUGUST 2002

MARITAL FLAWS

SIR – Sybil Ruscoe's article on the marital problems that are besetting certain members of England's cricket team merely underlines the pathetic and self-indulgent attitude that prevails in some of today's married women.

When Mesdames Butcher, Gough and Thorpe first met their husbands, there is no doubt that, quite naturally, they basked in the reflected glory that accompanying such men afforded them, and they would certainly have enjoyed the benefits of the association – charity dinners, fine restaurants and rubbing shoulders with the great and the good.

They were also aware that these men were no ordinary mortals, and that the specific nature of their jobs would inevitably mean long periods apart. The compensation for this would be a fair degree of financial security and the knowledge that, given the average life of a Test cricketer, their men would be affluent and more available by their mid-thirties.

Sixty years ago thousands of women in this country waved goodbye to their husbands for up to five years, and in many cases forever. Not for them a regular trip to Sainsbury's or Toys R Us with loads of plastic spending, but years of misery trying to put food on the table for the kids with stringent rationing and nightly visits from the Luftwaffe.

And before the advent of air travel, England's cricket team would spend three months at sea on a round trip to Australia, together with another three months trying to either defend or regain the Ashes. Not a whimper was heard from Mesdames Hutton, Compton, Graveney and Edrich, because they appreciated that the prime role within their marriages was to support their husbands.

It is bad enough when key players are lost through injury, but when the finest batsman of his generation is reduced to the level of a village-green cricketer because his wife couldn't wait for the dramatic improvement in her lifestyle five years hence, then the ECB will eventually be reduced to adopting a 'bachelors only' selection policy.

Tony Little
Dorking

6 SEPTEMBER 2002

BOWLERS' LOT

SIR – Mr Arnold Alcock writes (23 August) 'Alec Bedser and Fred Trueman did not play the number of matches the present-day cricketer plays'.

We certainly did not play as many international matches as a small number of first-class players today. I only wish I could have done so. Through no fault of my own I did not play any first-class cricket, or hardly any cricket at all, from 1940 to 1946 (age 22 to 28). Like thousands of others we spent months and years away from home in the Forces.

I think there are too many international matches and they are apt to become commonplace, but players want more money so it has to come from somewhere. The question is, do players play more cricket than my generation, as Arnold Alcock states?

At the Oval we played 34 three-day games (first-class) each year, that is 102 days, as well as extraneous matches. Some examples of my work rate: from May 1946 to August 1947 I bowled 2,983 overs, from May 1948 to August 1949 2,778 overs, from May 1950 to August 1951 2,892 overs.

In 1953, I bowled 1,253 overs and took 162 wickets at 16.67, including 39 wickets against Australia at 17.23. In all, I bowled well over 1,000 overs per season for ten seasons, and 958, 900 and 963 overs in the other years. I am informed that I bowled some 17,500 overs in 15 years.

In view of Mr Alcock's comments, I would be interested to

know how these figures compare with any England opening bowler in the last ten years. My only comment is I wish I could start again.

Alec Bedser
Woking

13 SEPTEMBER 2002

SIR – Why do so many current fast bowlers injure their knees and ankles?

Bedser and Trueman rarely missed a match. They wore proper boots, with ankle-supporting leather, as opposed to today's light 'shoes'. When they turned an ankle in footholds they had protection.

Similarly, young people then walked more than today. We walked to and from school, to parks and swimming pools – we were not taken everywhere by car. Thus our legs were stronger.

Robert Jackson
Sheffield

20 SEPTEMBER 2002
SUREFIRE STATHAM

SIR – For years I have screamed at the television set 'Make him play!' as England's bowlers greeted each new batsman with balls pitched short and way outside off stump. Not only have our bowlers not learnt anything, they are actually getting worse. Rock bottom was reached (we hope) in one session this summer when the Channel 4 scorer recorded the appalling fact that 44 per cent of England's deliveries had not required the Indian batsmen to play a stroke.

My thoughts turned to the man who most players and writers regarded as the most accurate pace bowler of all time, the late, great Brian Statham, whose motto was – if they miss, I hit. Although oversimplified as a philosophy, it was endorsed by the fact that nearly half of his victims in first-class cricket were clean bowled and if you add the lbws, an amazing 63 per cent of his 2,260 Test and county victims did not require the help of a fielder. And his average was 16.36.

Besides pace and accuracy, Statham's other attribute was his consistency; day in, day out, to the point where batsmen, in trying to escape his suffocating persistence, had to take their risks against his partners, Fred Trueman and Frank Tyson, thereby contributing to their impressive hauls.

Are there really no fast bowlers who can combine intelligence with a technique that will stand up to continuous work? Well, yes there are. Unfortunately, they tend to play for Australia.

Geoffrey Hollows
Yeovil

15 NOVEMBER 2002

BOWLERS ON SLIDE

SIR – Simon Jones damaged his knee sliding to stop the ball. This is common practice these days, and is it any wonder that so many English fast bowlers are prone to injury? Fast bowlers of Jones's calibre should be wrapped up in cotton wool and forbidden to dive. Place them at third man or deep fine leg, out of harm's way. Twenty or 30 years ago the likes of John Snow and Bob Willis wouldn't even deign to pick the ball up when it was knocked back to them by the batsman.

Mike Banyard
Charlton Adam

6 DECEMBER 2002

MORE PLAYERS

SIR – In Victorian times it was not unusual in cricket matches to redress a difference in class between two sides by increasing the number of players on the inferior side (for instance, in 1874 in Adelaide, W.G.'s XI played against 22 of South Australia).

In order to try to introduce a better level of competition in the remaining two Test matches, I suggest that the following format be used: the whole England squad against XI of Australia.

Ian A. Macgregor
Nairn

6 JUNE 2003

FOUL UP

SIR – The recent debate on swearing in pubs (report, 3 June) recalled a cricket club meeting, when it was proposed that they should try to persuade women to umpire. A committee member objected: 'But what about the language?'

The chairman replied: 'The players will just have to put up with it.'

V.L. Coombes
Bovey Tracey

7 AUGUST 2003

SIR – When I was at my prep school, admittedly some 80 odd years ago, only three players – the bowler, the wicketkeeper and, if necessary, the captain – were allowed to appeal.

More shouts automatically resulted in 'not out' (this did not apply in run outs). This ruling was enforced in all the schools against whom we played in south east London at that time.

'Sledging' was an unknown word.

John Charnaud
Feock

20 AUGUST 2003
FIXTURE JOKE

SIR – First-class cricket has become inaccessible. During the whole of August my local team, Northamptonshire, will play a grand total of two days' first-team cricket at home. For many sports fans the county game used to be an indispensable part of the summer, but I believe the present empty and irregular schedule is causing potential spectators to drift away.

Dick Rayment
Northampton

6 SEPTEMBER 2003
TERMS OF ART

SIR – Having once puzzled my wife by telling her that the Test cricketer Derek Underwood was an excellent night watchman, I now face the problem of explaining that the South African Paul Adams is a left-arm Chinaman.

Roy Larman
Salisbury

1 OCTOBER 2003
LESS THAN ZERO

SIR – I would like to ask Messrs Parkinson, Atherton and Willis (otherwise known as the Cricket Reform Group) how reducing the number of county championship cricket matches will improve the performance of Test match players. I don't understand how not playing in ten matches is better than not playing in 16.

Gary Beard
Brighton

21 APRIL 2004
LARA GOT IT RIGHT

SIR – Why were so many commentators criticising Brian Lara for batting on for personal glory when he could have instead declared to give the West Indies a better chance to win a dead rubber at the end of a lost series? How many people remember Len Hutton's 364? Who remembers the series score? How many people remember Sir Garfield Sobers's 365? Who remembers the series score?

I think Lara got it right. West Indies cricket will surely benefit far more in the long run from having the world record holder and the first batsman to score 400 than if they had won that last Test. Children emulate heroes, and losing a Test series 3–1 instead of 3–0 does not inspire anyone. Bravo Brian Lara – a true cricket legend.

Derek Brown
Ashford

WINE WHINE

SIR – I am shocked at the ban – which will include members – on bringing alcohol into cricket grounds which the International Cricket Council proposes introducing in 2006. Whoever thought this one up clearly does not understand what going to a cricket match is all about.

It is: good cricket, good company, good food and good wine. The menus for our three-course lunches include beef stroganoff, chicken korma, coronation chicken, asparagus wrapped in ham and poached salmon. How can you expect to have this fare without wine?

Incidentally, does this mean that the hospitality boxes will be unable to bring in alcoholic drinks either? It would be unfair if the prawn sandwich brigade get preference over members.

J.V. Addison OBE
Dalston

27 MAY 2004

MISSING THREE RUNS

SIR – The end of the Lord's Test (Comment, 26 May) superbly illustrated the absurdity of a bureaucratic change to the rules of cricket. When Nasser Hussain hit a four to win the match, the scores were level and he was on 102.

Thanks to the change of rule, he was credited only with the one run necessary to give England a win, so that his final score was not the 106 he actually made, but only 103. Imagine the outcry if he had hit his four when he was on 98 and thus been deprived by this daft rule of his century.

Christopher Booker
Litton

31 AUGUST 2004
FIELDING CALLS

SIR – The story of a tennis player on the mobile phone (27 August) reminded me of a Champagne moment during a local cricket match. One of our players was fielding out on the boundary, when the opposition batsman hit a huge shot high in the air towards him. Our team-mate calmly asked the friend he was talking to on his mobile to hold on and put the phone in his pocket. The ball descended, he took an excellent catch, then retrieved his phone and resumed his conversation as if nothing had happened.

Jim Strother
St Albans

2 SEPTEMBER 2004
ON A WING AND A PRAYER

SIR – I think I can cap Jim Strother's cricketing Champagne moment (31 August).

Towards the end of a long, hot afternoon at a match on the common at Tunbridge Wells, back in the early 1950s, one of Linden Park's deep fielders, vaguely conscious of having heard a loud click from the direction of the wicket, looked up to see a small, dark shape hurtling towards him. Instinctively his hand shot up, and in one of the neatest catches ever witnessed on the common, he caught a swallow.

Jonathan Goodall
Bath

3 SEPTEMBER 2004

SIR – I am lucky enough to be attending the ICC cricket final and was looking forward to packing a picnic. I received my tickets this week and, along with it, the amusing letter from David Clarke, the tournament director, thanking 'commercial partners' for their support and continuing: 'Non-alcoholic beverages (including water and soft drinks) not produced by Pepsi and crisps and snacks not produced by Walkers will not be permitted into the venue for matches during the tournament.'

I fully appreciate that cricket requires sponsorship to keep it solvent and vigorous, but this appears to be a step towards insanity. In years to come, will I be required to leave my Marks & Spencer's boxer shorts at the gate if BHS is a 'commercial partner'? Will my Orange mobile not work if Vodafone is a 'commercial partner'?

My generation is well used to branding and voluntarily sports logos and branded clothing. That is a choice. I was unaware that attending a cricket match, and paying handsomely for the privilege, required me to assign my own billboard rights and to become an approved hoarding for the 'commercial partners'.

Do I get paid for this I wonder? Should we also not all be members of Equity as bit-players in the televisual experience?

Paul Ferguson
London SW6

15 DECEMBER 2004

SIR – What an indictment of the myopic greed and poor judgment of the England and Wales Cricket Board that MCC should have to demand an urgent meeting to discuss the selling of television rights (10 December).

English cricket's policy and philosophy in this area, for the greater good of the game, should have been established in the infancy of satellite broadcasting.

The comments of Mike Gatting and Anthony Wreford in Sybil Ruscoe's report were spot on. Given the scarcity of proper, hard-ball cricket in state sector schools, terrestrial television coverage is essential to the game's future. Kwik-cricket is fine as far as it goes, but there are probably thousands of talented youngsters who never get any further and never pick up a real cricket bat or ball in earnest, especially with football now almost a year-round sport. They are lost to the game for ever.

I suppose, though, that when one's field of vision is filled with masses of pound signs, it's difficult to see anything else – even the obvious.

Paul Easterbrook
Stoke Hill
Exeter

PROPER COVERAGE

SIR – In the current furore no one seems to have considered the poor coverage of cricket by the terrestrial broadcasters.

Channel 4 and the BBC were happy to use it to pad out their daytime schedules, but after 4 p.m. *Countdown* and *Richard and Judy* took precedence. Saturdays were worse with horse racing interrupting the cricket.

The BBC considered it necessary to give us news (both local and national) and weather (likewise) hourly.

Sky Sports can be taken out only for the period of the Tests and at least then one gets proper coverage.

N.J. Binns
Burnham

28 DECEMBER 2004

HARD FACTS ABOUT SNOW AND CRICKET

SIR – Martin Hall (23 December) is incorrect in his statement that there was a snowfall in north Kent on 1 June, 1976. In fact, the remarkably late snowfall occurred on 2 June, 1975, when snow was reported at many locations in the British Isles as far south as Manston.

The Daily Telegraph of 3 June, 1975, gave full coverage to this extraordinarily unseasonal snowfall, and published what has become a classic photograph of a couple of disconsolate spectators sitting at the snowbound cricket pitch at Buxton awaiting the commencement of the match between Derbyshire and Lancashire. Snow stopped play all day.

Norman Brooks
Fellow of the Royal Meteorological Society
Costessey
Norwich

26 JANUARY 2005
ARMY DISSERVICE

SIR – It's tea on the fourth day of the fifth Test at Centurion. My enjoyment of the day's play so far has been made possible by the absence of the 'Barmy Army'. This element of so-called British supporters are proving to be the scourge of British cricket with their persistent pollution of grounds across the world and thousands of homes of real cricket lovers in the UK.

If they were real supporters, they would have been there today at the start of play. I suspect that later in the day, when they have sobered up, I will have to turn off the sound of my TV and miss the much-appreciated comments of the commentary team.

I can't understand why Mr Lloyd speaks with deference, tolerance and even affection, of this intemperate crowd.

As I close, the 'Barmy Army' have returned, as I suspected. Roll on Lord's.

Neville Fisher
Cardiff

2 FEBRUARY 2005

ARMY NOT BARMY

SIR – I wonder if Mr Fisher (26 January) has experienced a cricket tour and what he considers to be a 'real cricket lover'. May I point out a few things about the Barmy Army or 'scourge of British cricket': we are real cricket supporters who are there at the start of play, and are most definitely not an 'intemperate crowd'. The Barmy Army is not an exclusive club – many English supporters on arranged tours join us to sing and enjoy cricket banter. We raise a large amount of money for charity – most recently towards the tsunami relief fund.

Michael Vaughan and other members of the England team often describe us as the '12th man' when they spend long, hot days in the field and we are known to lift their spirits. The team clearly value our efforts. The Barmy Army's aim is to make watching cricket more fun and more popular – this is truly being fulfilled.

Marie Fidler
Chesterfield

4 MARCH 2005

DIGITAL REPLAY

SIR – The delay in digital signals (3 March) can be beneficial to the satellite viewer. You can read a book while listening to cricket commentary on the radio and when a wicket falls you have about one and a half seconds to look up at the television and see it fall live.

Neil Kershaw
Royton

15 APRIL 2005
CUT THE CLICHÉ

SIR – When will it be possible for certain journalists to write about the Marylebone Cricket Club without reference to the inaccurate and outdated image exemplified by Simon Briggs's daft remark (8 April) about 'red-faced reactionaries spluttering about the end of the Empire'? The reopening of the magnificently refurbished Pavilion at Lord's last week, attended by young and old, male and female, cutting edge and traditional, was a marvellous occasion that illustrated perfectly MCC's ability to move with the times and to embrace all kinds of cricket lovers. The wildly unoriginal attempt to be amusing merely illustrates that it is he who has become a cliché from yesteryear, not MCC.

Tim Rice
President MCC (2002–03)

27 APRIL 2005
GLOOMY OUTLOOK

SIR – I have been a cricket player and fan all my life. I am so disgusted with what is available to me that I think this year is the last I will pay my county membership.

The fixture list is dreadful: first-class cricket is jammed into the dodgy-weather periods at the start and end of the season, and the good-weather period taken up by endless beer matches.

The game is so besotted with the idea of getting new customers that it totally ignores the preferences of existing ones.

Roger Green
London SE25

4 MAY 2005

THE CATS' WHISKERS

SIR – Roger Green's letter had a profound impact on me. It so described my own anger at the way cricket is being turned into a sloggers' carnival that I decided to name my cat's new kittens Roger and Green.

In ten years' time, when these two little balls of fluff have grown into magnificent mousing machines, I'll be reminded that there was at least one other person who understood the value of our unique and magnificent county cricket.

Steve Baldock
Handcross

REPORT DUCKED THE HELMET EFFECT

SIR – With reference to the 'Amiss Helmet' comments by Simon Briggs (28 April), I am aware that lack of space can lead to important subjects receiving short measure. However, the single paragraph describing the 'helmet effect' is too inaccurate to pass muster in any circumstances.

'Legitimising short-pitched bowling' is incorrect. 'Brought the hook stroke into common currency' is way wide of the leg stump. 'Changed the way the game is played' hardly tells the story.

If Simon has the space, time or inclination to broaden the debate I am sure there are any number of pre-helmet players who will be happy to discuss the matter in more depth – including me.

Ted Dexter
Nice
France

NOT CRICKET?

SIR – Max Davidson's otherwise excellent piece 'Cricket's not a game, it's a metaphor for life' (Features, 21 May) is marred by the line 'Absurdly, my 14-year-old daughter has taken up cricket'.

Women were the first to play in white in 1745; we've had a national team since 1933; the women's and girls' game is a growth area throughout most of the UK; the current national team has had a run of one-day internationals and Test victories over the past three years that should make the men's squad blush.

What's absurd about that?

Catherine Rose
Chair
Women's Cricket Advisory Group (ECB)
Olney
Buckinghamshire

PAYING THE DEBT

SIR – Fascinating stuff about the Four Great Living Yorkshiremen (Sport, 19 July). The other day I called in for the first time in years at Bradford League club Farsley's Red Lane ground, where 50 years ago Ray Illingworth and I played in the same junior team. And there was the great man himself, cutting the field and preparing the pitch just as he has done for some years.

I wonder just how many former Test or county captains are putting back so much into the game, paying off some of the debt they owe to the club where they spent their formative years.

David Swallow
Pool-in-Wharfedale

26 AUGUST 2005

CRUCIAL TIME LOST

SIR – The playing restrictions in the current Test series have meant that most days so far have failed to see the full 90 overs being bowled. By insisting that play must end at 6 p.m., Channel 4 arguably deprived England of the few crucial extra overs necessary to win the last Test. Sky give all sports the full coverage that terrestrial television have no interest in providing.

Mark Purdy
Bishop's Stortford

27 AUGUST 2005

THE CRICKET TEST

SIR – In his column, Andrew O'Hagan (25 August) makes a gratuitously offensive reference to 'Norman Tebbit's obnoxious cricket test'.

What is obnoxious about noticing whether immigrants or their children integrate sufficiently to commit themselves to the country to which they have come, or whether socially and culturally they remain committed to the country they left to seek a better life?

What I found obnoxious were racist young Asians who jeered Nasser Hussain because he was captain of England.

Lord Tebbit
London SW1

30 AUGUST 2005

SIR – At the Albert Hall, the news leaked out that England had won the Test match. Six thousand people burst into deafening applause. I am sure Lord Tebbit would have been very proud of us.

Timothy Mundy
Croydon
Surrey

SIR – Andrew Cave (City Life, 27 August) suggests that this Ashes series could do for county cricket what Gazza and the soccer World Cup did for club football in the early 1990s. I think not, as there is one huge difference. If you went to White Hart Lane in 1990, there was every chance of seeing Paul Gascoigne play. If you go to Old Trafford to watch Lancashire in a county championship game expecting to see Andrew Flintoff play, there is every chance, thanks to 'central contracts', that you will be disappointed.

Neil Kershaw
Royton

2 SEPTEMBER 2005
CRICKET OUTDATED

SIR – Why doesn't cricket meet the challenges of the 21st century? Have a batting team and a bowling/fielding team (similar to American baseball), with a defined number of innings. Who wants to watch tailenders batting, or specialist batsmen sending over trundlers? Wouldn't it be more fun to watch six, seven or eight specialist batsmen taking on five, six or seven specialist bowlers in a true contest between bat and ball? The sports spectator these days wants to see a quality spectacle, with a result that is determined within a reasonable time frame. Still, I suppose something like that is too revolutionary for the dinosaur administrators that inhabit the world of cricket.

Bill Marczak
Sydney
Australia

7 SEPTEMBER 2005
NOT CRICKET

SIR – There are few things England's cricket-loving gentry enjoy more than ridiculing what they clearly perceive as the plebeian vulgarity of Association football and all its works.

Yet now it seems the ECB is planning to celebrate the hoped-for England Ashes victory with the kind of triumphalist, open-topped bus tour routinely indulged in by cup-winning football teams.

Even to consider such an event is not just the kiss of death to England's chances at the Oval – it is simply 'not cricket'.

Robert Sharr
Hornchurch

12 SEPTEMBER 2005
NO CRICKET PLEASE, WE'RE ENGLISH

SIR – Lord Deedes argues (Comment, 9 September) that the loss of millions of viewers of England's cricket team over the next few years – because of the exclusive Sky TV deal – will be offset by the extra money generated to nurture the game at grassroots level.

Unfortunately, a lot of that money is going to be wasted by

giving it to schools, when it should be given to clubs who can provide adequate facilities with the remit of fostering cricket as an extracurricular activity.

Furthermore, millions of youngsters are going to be denied the sight of Flintoff, Harmison, Pietersen, Vaughan continuing their astounding run of success. What young cricketers want is a sight of heroes in action, not the chance of playing an hour's quick-cricket in the playground once in a while.

David Belchamber
Barton-on-Sea

13 SEPTEMBER 2005

SIR – I am the proud owner of a new MCC cricket cap, purchased in the members' shop in the Pavilion at Lord's, clearly marked 'Made in Australia'.

Peter West
Bosham

15 SEPTEMBER 2005

SIR – When I got married in 1955 my husband told me he was going to give me the greatest thrill a girl could have on her honeymoon; he took me to Lord's.

Joyce Mantell
Tamworth

9 DECEMBER 2005

FROM ASHES TO DUST

SIR – Well, well, well. How the mighty England cricket team have fallen. From Ashes heroes to touring duds. All we could hear down here in Australia after the Ashes series was how England would become the new 'Australia' and dominate world cricket for a decade.

What a laugh. Scraping through an Ashes series 2–1 against a side who were performing well below their usual standards, your side were riding on the wave of desperate public emotion. Your whole country was desperate for Ashes glory. In Pakistan, against an ordinary Pakistan side (who were thrashed in January of this year by Australia, by the way), your glory boys were (as Kevin Pietersen would put it) annihilated by Pakistan.

Your guys are a long way from being the best side in the world. They're skilful and talented for the most part but do not have the mental capabilities to win consistently around the world in all conditions.

I even heard Duncan Fletcher complaining that the hotel environment on tour in Pakistan was detrimental to his team's mental state. Why don't you give Ricky Ponting or Steve Waugh a call and get a lesson on mental toughness.

Matt Ryan
Sydney
Australia

29 DECEMBER 2005
CHANGING CRICKET

SIR – Has cricket benefited from Kerry Packer's bank-rolling of what was then seen as revolution in a sleepy sport, or not (Comment, 28 December)?

Way ahead of his time, Packer was alive to the commercial upside of the one-day, guaranteed-result game, and generated box office. Perhaps he introduced cricket to millions who previously had not enjoyed, or had time for, the long form of the game. Perhaps he put bums on seats, which created revenue streams that allowed for the game to improve in standard through coaching, facilities and regularity of high-quality fixtures. Perhaps he moved (some) journalists covering matches from the bar to the press box because people wanted to see and hear of the great deeds of Botham, Lloyd, Richards and Wasim, whether in pyjamas or not. Good on yer, Kerry: hope you made money from it. Cricket has.

Ed Atkinson
Old Heathfield

16 JANUARY 2006
HOLY BATSMAN

SIR – The obituary of Gerry Hollis (13 January) brought back happy memories of the time he was my parish priest in Rossington and we both played in the village cricket team. A wedding early on a Saturday afternoon didn't stop him playing. After the service, he would jump on to his bicycle and ride to the ground, where he would dash into the pavilion and whip off his cassock to reveal immaculate whites underneath. A change of footwear and, if we'd lost the toss, he was ready to field.

George Horne
Escrick

24 JANUARY 2006
HONOURS DISGRACE

SIR – Awarding the whole England cricket team an MBE or OBE is a disgrace. Players who have fewer than ten Test caps, 1,000 runs, 100 wickets have been honoured when true greats such as Gower, Botham, Gooch and Willis had to wait years to be recognised. Will they all be knighted if they retain the Ashes in Australia in 12 months' time?

Martin Clements
Wokingham

24 MARCH 2006
LEAVE LORD'S ALONE

SIR – I have to disagree with Giles Clarke's ideas about 50,000-seat cricket stadiums (23 March). The Oval maybe, but Lord's, with its charm and variety of stands, has always been rightly considered by the MCC to be a cricket ground, not a stadium. Tiered stands towering ever upwards might bring in more dosh, but would irrevocably destroy the essence of Lord's.

John Fiddy
Great Hockham

19 MAY 2006
FLETCHER AT FAULT

SIR – Further to Derek Pringle's comment (17 May) about practising slip catches from a left-handed batsman (Duncan Fletcher), surely the problem is more fundamental. It is one thing to take a catch in practice when you have every reason to expect it and another to take the one chance that might come your way in a full day's play.

Most members of the Test team have only played one-day cricket recently, where slip catching is more or less redundant.

They would have benefited from playing some four-day county cricket as a warm-up to the Test series. It was noticeable that the only close fielder who caught his catches was

Marcus Trescothick, who beforehand had been playing county cricket for Somerset.

David Hancorn
Woodley

GIVE KNITTING A SPORTING CHANCE

SIR – I have spent hours knitting cricket sweaters while watching my husband and son play cricket.

Last Sunday, the Vine at Hambledon (the home of cricket) played a friendly match against Denmead. The first half was played with much interaction from the boundary, as we settled down with our picnics, only to be interrupted by the England versus Ecuador match on the pavilion television, which we all watched.

The second half resumed after the football match, with the Vine winning the trophy. A good time was had by all.

If your correspondent Angela Moghabghab (26 June) is short of knitting projects, the British and International Sailors' Society distributes 10,000 woolly hats each year and we could always do with more.

She could knit a hat or two while watching Wimbledon.

Jan Webber
Hambledon

SIR – One of my cats, sadly deceased, was called Geoffrey. We referred to him as Geoffrey Boycat – my husband being a Yorkshireman and keen cricketer.

Poor old Geoff used up many of his nine lives – for the last four years of his life he only had three legs, but could still chase for the kill. My husband then referred to him as Wicket, which was a bit cruel.

Sue Baines
Quernmore

14 JULY 2006

DOBBER FINDS THE PERFECT LENGTH
TO DISMISS HUGHES

SIR – I could not help a smile when I read an article in the sports pages by your expert analyst Simon Hughes (15 May). He wrote: 'If you look at footage of pre-War Test cricket, most batsmen lingered on the back foot dabbing and nurdling the ball against wily trundlers on pitches barely discernible from the outfield. The sun never shone [how did he know?]. This strip [for England's match against Sri Lanka at Lord's earlier this month] is firm and trustworthy and only tinged with green, but some of the old dobbers – a Shackleton or a Bedser – might have utilised the conditions well.'

I would point out to Simon Hughes that one of those old 'dobbers' did go to Australia in 1950–51 and took 30 wickets at 16.06 in five Tests – there were no green tinges of green grass there. In the next series the old 'dobber', also against Australia in five Test matches, did take 39 wickets at 17.00 each. A matter of 69 wickets in ten consecutive games versus Australia at less than 17.00 each. From 1950 to 1953 this old 'dobber' did take 121 Test wickets in 21 Tests at 18.16 each. Not bad for an old 'dobber'. Perhaps we might find another one somewhere. The sun did shine in those days, despite Simon Hughes's comment. I don't suppose your analyst saw the 'dobber' bowl – he's not old enough to have done so.

Alec Bedser
Woking

21 JULY 2006
TALES OF TRUEMAN

SIR – Geoffrey Boycott's piece on Fred Trueman (3 July) contains inaccuracies. Firstly, I never addressed Fred as 'Trueman'. Had I done so, he would never have spoken to me again.

Secondly, the good-humoured exchange followed Yorkshire's win over Leicestershire at Sheffield in 1968, in which Fred, who also happened to be captaining the side at the time on account of injury to Brian Close, took six for twenty in the second innings. This was to be Fred's last season and even he had begun to realise that his considerable powers were on the wane. This failed to prevent his boasting of the ways in which he had dismissed Leicestershire's batsmen, demonstrating ball by ball how one had swung away late, the next one nipped back, and so on.

This prompted my mischievous question of whether he had bowled a 'straight ball'. He was somewhat taken aback, but retorted: 'Aye, it were a full toss to Peter Marner and went straight through 'im like a streak of p*** and knocked out his middle stump!'

'Sobers' – incidentally, Fred would always accord his fellow giant of the game the respect of the prefix Gary – was nothing whatever to do with the proceedings.

Incidentally, there was a follow-up question from me, which was not reported: 'Fred, would you describe yourself as a modest man?' Sadly, he did not live long enough to furnish an answer.

Richard Hutton
Wetherby

28 JULY 2006

ROBERTSON'S RIPOSTE

SIR – Peter Clarke (21 July) did not mention the consequence of the selectors' decision (when they dropped Jack Robertson in favour of the more established Cyril Washbrook after Robertson had made 121 in a Test match at Lord's). While England then went on to play in yet another drawn game at Manchester, my father made his record 331 not out on the first day at Worcester. This allowed Middlesex to declare on 623 for five and win by an innings and 54 runs.

Ian Robertson
Bury St Edmunds

23 AUGUST 2006

TIME FOR A REDESIGNED CRICKET BALL

SIR – The conventional cricket ball is way past its sell-by date. I speak as a former fast left-arm bowler who had the nasty experience of knocking a batsman's teeth out with the first ball of a university match, because it was wet.

Surely with materials technology, we can reinvent the ball with built-in swing features to avoid the need for tampering.

I would think that a Formula One technical team such as McLaren could produce a modern, safer high-tech ball in space-age materials.

Colin Calvert
Ampthill

1 SEPTEMBER 2006

SIR – In my much younger days in club cricket I came up against a very well known county player who in his retirement played some club cricket. Batting second I was amazed at how much swing even an old 'pro' could get on a ball already 160 runs old. All was revealed when I managed to look at the ball, which was shiny bright on one side. He told me afterwards that he had a lump of wax stuck on the instep of his boot and when convenient he transferred some to the ball and gave it a polish. This was in the 1950s, so there is nothing new about 'ball tampering'.

Ronald Head
Dumbleton

13 OCTOBER 2006
DISAPPEARING OVERS

SIR – Professional Cricketers' Association members have backed a proposal to reduce from 104 to 96, the number of overs bowled each day in first-class cricket (7 October).

Lord MacLaurin started the trend, reducing the overs from 112 to 104. I don't recall him asking his employees at Tesco, when he was chairman, if they wanted a reduction in their working day without a reduction in pay.

Neil Kershaw
Royton

24 NOVEMBER 2006
BIGGER AND BETTER

SIR – With reference to the story of the two young Indian cricketers who amassed 721 runs in a single partnership, allowing their team to claim a record victory of 700 runs. In fact, this is not the biggest margin of victory. This honour goes to Pakistan Railways. In December 1964 in the Ayub Trophy, batting first, the Railways scored 910 for six declared. They then dismissed their opponents, Dera Ismail Khan, for 32 and 27 to win by an innings and 851 runs.

Also of note in the Pakistan Railways innings was the score of Pervez Akhtar, who made 337 not out, his maiden century, and also a world record highest maiden hundred.

Ray Pearce
Castle Bromwich

8 DECEMBER 2006
DARK DAYS FOR GILES

SIR – All the cricket correspondents I have read have got it wrong. The second Test, and possibly the Ashes, was not lost on the final day. It was lost when Ashley Giles dropped Ricky Ponting in Australia's first innings. As a matter of interest, I would like to know whether the sunglasses Giles was wearing would have any impact, positive or negative, in assisting his vision while fielding.

Roy Deal
Locks Heath

27 DECEMBER 2006
JEEVES'S CREASE

SIR – The tailors Gieves and Hawkes might have enjoyed the patronage of such well-dressed men as Bertie Wooster, but would be shocked at the allegation that they inspired the name of his manservant (Travel, 23 December).

They would surely know that Jeeves was named after the Warwickshire cricketer Percy Jeeves (1888–1916), whom P.G. Wodehouse saw play at Cheltenham in 1912. Wodehouse confirmed this and added that he was following the example of

Arthur Conan Doyle, who liked naming his characters after professional cricketers.

N.T.P. Murphy
London N11

29 DECEMBER 2006
CUT OF HIS FLANNELS, MARK OF THE MAN

SIR – P.G. Wodehouse may have been inspired to name Bertie Wooster's manservant after seeing Percy Jeeves playing cricket in 1912 (27 December), but one wonders if the choice was prompted by his prowess, or the cut of his flannels.

In the early years of the 20th century, white trousers were essential kit for participants and observers of many sports, including cricket, tennis, yachting and rowing. As the fifth generation of my family to be engaged in our tailoring business, I know Gieves & Hawkes, renowned for an understanding of correct dress, included 'whites' in its gentleman's catalogue for 1911.

Perhaps Wodehouse appreciated the natural link between performance and style, and saw good reason to choose the name Jeeves for a character accomplished in all the necessities.

Robert Gieve
London W1

SIR – With this latest performance from the English cricket team, I trust that, on their return to London, they will be driven round London in an open-topped bus to enable us to boo them.

R.P. Rankine
Quinta dos Arcos
Portugal

5 JANUARY 2007

COMIC DIVERSION

SIR – Can one read any significance into the BBC's decision to screen *Steptoe & Son,* and then *Grumpy Old Men,* instead of the Ashes highlights when there was no play on the final two days of the fourth Test? Do the programme schedulers have a sense of humour?

Nigel Allsop
London W14

8 JANUARY 2007

PUT TO FLIGHT

SIR – Following the triumphant open-topped bus tour through London in 2005, should the England cricket team be made to fly home from Australia in an open-topped plane?

Dr S. McMenemin
Coylton

6 APRIL 2007

HATS OFF TO THE 'FLINTOFF' OF HIS GENERATION

SIR – The recent Flintoff fracas called to mind the successful Hampshire side of 50 or so years ago. Their captain, Colin Ingleby-Mackenzie, widely renowned for his nocturnal revelry, cricket or no cricket, was appointed captain of a team which went to the West Indies under the management of the late Jim Swanton.

Swanton insisted that the players should be in bed by 11. But Ingleby-Mackenzie objected. To the amazement of all he opined that 11 was madness – much too late. The matches were due to start at 11.30, he reminded them.

A.H. Green
Bedford

18 MAY 2007

VARIETY WAS NOT THE ONLY SPICE OF O'GORMAN'S LIFE

SIR – Thank you for including my dad, Joe O'Gorman, in your list of cricketers with other things in their life (Sport, 12 May). By 1927, Dad had already been working the variety halls as a versatile and increasingly well-known act for 20 years. He was 36 when he played for Surrey, having worked his way up through club cricket with Richmond and Honor Oak, and practice at the Oval with the professionals (members could get a net there in those days), Surrey Club and Ground, and Surrey 2nd XI.

Cricket was his passion and relaxation from the world of theatre, travelling the circuits around the country week by week. He was determined to reach the highest level and constantly practised his leg breaks and googlies (one which could be picked and another which could not). He was a consummate bowler. He had length, flight, variation of pace and used sliders and top spinners, which are not unknown today. He also averaged 104 with the bat in his Surrey matches in teams which included Hobbs, Fender, Jardine, Ducat, Strudwick, Sandham and Gover – England cricketers all.

Though he was picked for two more matches he had to decline as he and his brother, Dave, were booked to appear in Liverpool and Newcastle and obviously his work had to come first.

Brian O'Gorman
West Sussex

22 JUNE 2007
BETTER OFF AT HOME

SIR – My wife and I haven't attended a Test match for over 15 years because we weren't prepared to sit next to foul-mouthed yobs, trumpeters and drunks, none of whom seemed to be interested in cricket. Now we watch at home in peace and in comfort, thoroughly enjoying the experience and seeing all the key moments in detail.

Our year's subscription to Sky Sports costs us less than a single day's Test cricket for two, given the cost of travel, food and admission. And we don't have the hassle of getting home afterwards!

John Gardner
Winchester

1 JUNE 2007
FOUR THOUGHT NEEDED

SIR – The injury to Ramnaresh Sarwan highlights the absurdity and danger of the 'Is it a four or not?' rule. Frequently we see a player contort himself to an unnatural degree to ensure that no part of the body is touching the boundary rope.

Technology then takes over and we have 'x' number of replays. Why bother? Surely if a player prevents the ball from reaching the boundary that should be sufficient and a miraculous save should not be denied by a fraction of flannel or an errant toecap.

R.S. Ayers
London SE18

CATCHING DISEASE

SIR – I think it is about time for a new Law in cricket. Every time the ball goes in the air these days, the wicketkeeper invariably shouts 'Catch it!' This is clearly not simply a reminder to fielders that if they catch the ball, the batsman is out – you would think that they are well aware of that already. No, it is pure gamesmanship: an attempt to influence the umpire into believing that the ball came off the bat.

My proposal is that if anyone on the fielding side shouts 'Catch it!', the umpire should immediately say, 'Not out'.

Joe Kerrigan
London W13

CONTRACTS ARE KILLERS

SIR – While a long-time admirer of Derek Pringle's writing, along with I suspect nearly every first-class cricketer of my generation, I read with a wry smile his thoughts on the crop of injuries to England's Test match bowlers.

Far from the England medical staff being 'careless' in preventing these, there's one simple explanation: Harmison, Jones, Hoggard, Flintoff, Giles etc may be considered as 'fit' in the all-round definition of the word – but are they fit to bowl? Certainly not. Why?

Central contracts originally led to them being pulled out of the county cricket programme, ensuring they didn't bowl enough overs. As the late Tom Cartwright (a 1,000-overs-a-season man) aptly put it: 'I bowl myself fit to bowl!'

As Derek Pringle wrote, that otherwise admirable coach Duncan Fletcher made a crucial mistake by 'wrapping his players in cotton wool'. That's the very last thing a cricketer needs. You cannot hold form or confidence by endless net practice or resting up at home. In cricket – as in most sports – the 'cooking's' done in the kitchen cauldron of the game itself.

And as for Kevin Pietersen's claim that he's been 'over-worked of late', it's a shame he didn't experience two three-day matches a week plus a charity game on Sundays, every week for four months; no motorway travel between venues and staying in down-market three-star hotels – all for a wage no current car park attendant would work for! Then he'd have a point worth listening to.

Peter Walker
(Glamorgan & England 1956–1972),
Llandaff

3 AUGUST 2007
SET BETTER EXAMPLE

SIR – On Tuesday I umpired an under-15 cricket match and there was incessant chatter from both the fielding sides. The sledging got more and more personal and in the end I had to intervene and ask that the match continue with less verbal involvement.

Like all youngsters they copy their elders and alleged betters, and until the ECB seem really committed to their 'Spirit of Cricket' campaign then bad behaviour will continue right through the game. Future umpires will find their job almost impossible.

H.D. Smith
Beckenham

31 AUGUST 2007

THE DAY MY BOSS LET ME WITNESS
THE END OF AN ERA

SIR – Fifty years ago, on Friday, 30 August, 1957, Denis Compton, aged 39, played his final innings as a professional cricketer for Middlesex. I was privileged to be there. The match was against Worcestershire and, on the first day, Compton scored 143. At the end of the second day, the match was evenly poised, with both sides having declared their first innings.

It was at this point that I decided I had to be there for the final day. However, taking a day's leave at short notice was frowned on at my office, and I was too honest to take a sickie.

The next morning, I approached my manager with my request. 'We only allow leave to be taken at such short notice for exceptional reasons,' he said. 'Well,' I replied, 'it's Denis Compton's last day in first-class cricket. Does that count?' He agreed it did, so I ran from the building and caught the train to St John's Wood.

I arrived in good time and saw Compton walk to the wicket with the score at 61 for two. During the next hour he scored 48 runs out of 70 added; a cameo of the first innings with all the shots that he played so well: the cover drive, going down the wicket before the ball was bowled, sometimes late-cutting from yards down the wicket, and, of course, the sweep. His innings ended with a spectacular catch at long-on. It was typical of Denis that he applauded the fielder on his way back, with everyone in the ground cheering. As he disappeared from view, it seemed like the end of an era.

Peter Clarke
Epsom

2 NOVEMBER 2007

HIRST FEAT WILL BE A HARD ACT TO FOLLOW

SIR – I am afraid in your report on the possibility of Muttiah Muralitharan surpassing Shane Warne's Test wicket-taking record (26 October) you wrongly attributed a famous cricket saying about surpassing milestones to Fred Trueman. The real source was George Hirst, the great Yorkshire and England all-rounder who, in 1906, took more than 200 wickets and scored over 2,000 runs in one season. When asked if he thought anyone would equal this feat, George replied: 'I don't know, but whoever does will be bloody tired.'

This was when the county championship was of some substance, and not the meaningless travesty that it is today.

M. Aldred
Wakefield

JUST NOT CRICKET

SIR – Now that the heavy rollers and sightscreens have been put away for the winter, is it not time for our cricketing author-ities to admit that after pandering to the demands of television to provide entertainment rather than sport, we now have two games?

First, we have real cricket – white flannels and traditional rules that have made it the finest game in the world. And now we have 'quicket' – very animated and vocal players in multi-coloured pyjamas performing in very quick games with supporting pop music.

It is a formula designed to attract and keep viewers with a very low attention span.

R. Mann
Bideford

TESTING US TOO MUCH

SIR – With regard to the proposals now under consideration to increase still further the amount of Test cricket played around the world, Hutber's Law has been forgotten together with the realisation that caviar for dinner every day will inevitably have us calling for baked beans instead sooner or later. Ashes to ashes.

Kenneth Wood
Exeter

EVANS SETS EXAMPLE

SIR – The failure of the England cricket team is a loss of nerve by the various England coaches. I always watch the performance of the wicketkeeper intently, since I first saw Godfrey Evans (before he played for England). On the 1946–47 tour of Australia, Godfrey replaced Paul Gibb (who was an opening bat) because the England team realised that if you dropped Bradman he was likely to score another 200-plus runs. The present England selectors seem to think that a keeper scoring 50 or 60 can somehow offset a dropped catch which enables a batsman to move on from 100 to 200! Let's face it, in Tests getting wickets is usually harder than scoring runs.

D.A.E. Fey
Bristol

KEEPERS WHO STOOD UP TO FAST BOWLERS

SIR – Derek Pringle writes (7 February) that it was Jack Russell who first used standing up to pace bowlers in one-day cricket.

I'm not sure if he was talking of limited-over cricket or the fact that a wicketkeeper was standing up to a lively fast-medium bowler – suggesting it was something new. Radio commentators always make a comment when a keeper stands up to pace, as though it was something recently adopted.

It may be of interest that Bert Strudwick, the great Surrey keeper both pre the 1914–18 Great War and up to 1926, stood up to most fast-medium bowlers. Struddy took some 1,400 victims and played his first Test against Australia in 1911 at Sydney. Maurice Tate, a great lively fast-medium bowler, always had Struddy standing up.

I saw a picture of the Test in 1924–25 with Struddy standing up to Tate. There were three slips and a gully standing some 20 yards back, giving some idea of Tate's nip off the pitch. Tich Cornford, of Sussex, always stood up to Tate.

Since 1947, Godfrey Evans (Kent) and Arthur McIntyre (Surrey) always stood up to me. They were great keepers and only went back if it was a really spiteful pitch. Back then, we played on uncovered pitches, so it was not easy standing up.

I had no idea of my speed in m.p.h. It didn't matter as long as I bowled a good length and direction and made the ball move. I'm sure the keeper standing up helped my bowling: I was lucky to have two great keepers.

Sir Alec Bedser CBE
Woking

14 MARCH 2008

KOLPAK TESTS ENGLAND

SIR – Following the debacle of the first Test defeat in Hamilton, is it any wonder England are sliding down the ratings of world cricket? Leicestershire recently announced their fifth Kolpak signing for the new season while Northamptonshire are also inundated with South African imports. One wonders if these counties have any interest in nurturing young English players for the future of international cricket.

Nigel Clarke
Swansea

19 APRIL 2008
TWENTY20 SOMETHING

SIR – I believe that Twenty20 cricket should be re-named to differentiate it from proper cricket.

How about 'whackit'?

John Bradford
Gosport

2 MAY 2008
EYES OF A HAWK

SIR – I read with great interest Derek Pringle's article regarding the potentially increased use of Hawk-Eye technology in cricket (1 May). Could an initial step not be to have a camera set for detecting front-foot no-balls, with the umpire receiving a signal to an ear piece? If umpires could concentrate purely on the flight of the ball and the goings on at the 'business end' of the pitch, their ability to make correct decisions would surely be enhanced. This would, I assume, be quite easy to set up and administer, and would also satisfy Peter Willey's call for the umpire to make on-field decisions, as it would just take away another line decision from the umpire.

Steve Bradbury
Droitwich Spa

12 MAY 2008

THE JOYS OF STREET CRICKET

SIR – The picture on the Letters page (9 May) brings back happy memories of carefree days in the car-free roads of the villages of County Durham, where we played cricket in the streets. A tennis ball was used to protect householders' windows, and a dustbin, propped up by a brick, took the place of stumps.

Powerful hooks into nearby gardens brought different rewards – 'one and in or six and out'. Happy days!

Reverend Fred Stainthorpe
Willenhall

30 MAY 2008

COLD COMFORT

SIR – Sitting on the boundary for four days of the second Test against New Zealand at Old Trafford, there was great *schadenfreude* watching the England players freezing in the field in their cheap and sloppy, new 'wonder kit'.

The opposition, the Black Caps, meanwhile simply called for their long-sleeved cable-knit sweaters and, I would imagine, were not only warmer but considerably smarter.

The piles of replica kit sales in the Old Trafford cricket store perhaps demonstrated the real reason why the England Cricket Board has welcomed the new kit with open arms.

Brian J. Singleton
Baslow

GIVE BOWLERS THE RIGHT TO SWITCH TOO

SIR – May I propose that rather than contemplate banning the Kevin Pietersen switch-hit, surely the equitable solution is not to ban an enterprising and skilful shot, but to allow the bowler a similar option to use either hand to deliver the ball.

It may take a little practice (but so does the switch-hit) and perhaps there would not be many bowlers capable of bowling with either arm. However, it is possible as I tried it many years ago, with a fair degree of accuracy, using a quick change of hands.

An even greater degree of surprise may be achieved by using the strategy of bowling off the wrong foot with the wrong hand, though this will take more practice. It would certainly give the game an extra dimension.

Malcolm Burley
Painswick

TWENTY20 WILL PASS

SIR – Professional cricket isn't lovely any more, sadly. Success is to be measured by increasing financial rewards. When the novelty of the 20-over game wears off, however – and it won't take long – the traditional game will still continue at clubs across the country. This is the stuff of headlines on the back pages of local newspapers and in schools, where the prizes are colours and the status that goes with them. All is not lost. Not yet.

Kenneth Wood
Exeter

27 JUNE 2008

THREAT TO CRICKET

SIR – Enjoy your Test and county cricket while you can. Soon the authorities will be reducing the number of county matches for us to watch, which will probably be followed by a reduction in the number of days per match.

This will eventually lead to the demise of county cricket as we know it, which in turn will sound the death knell of Test cricket.

We will then be left to watch them playing 'English baseball' in coloured pyjamas.

Eric Bradford
North Wootton

15 JULY 2008

BOMBS AWAY

SIR – As a friend and cricketing colleague of Bryan 'Bomber' Wells, I was privileged to share countless hours of his expertise on the pitch, and hilarious reminiscences off it. He certainly deserved the extensive and joyful obituary (11 July).

One omitted story was the occasion on which Bryan phoned the Kremlin and attempted to reverse the charges.

He enjoyed the whimsical suggestion that, when a bemused Kremlin operator was asked to put Bomber Wells through to Comrade Secretary General, Russia might have been placed on full military alert.

David Turner
West Bridgford

4 AUGUST 2008

SIR – County cricket teams have been very good at providing pairs of players. Kent had House and Key, Surrey had Tudor and Stewart, while Durham currently offer Mustard and Onions.

Darrell Farrant
Radcliffe on Trent

7 AUGUST 2008
THE CRYING GAME

SIR – I was disappointed by the vitriolic tone with which Judith Woods expressed her contempt for any man who cries (Features, 5 August).

It was clear that the former England cricket captain, Michael Vaughan, was struggling to contain his emotions. He was, after all, relinquishing the highest position of his profession.

I would like to live in a society where a man may express himself without fear of being labelled a sissy or having his masculinity questioned. A man cries because he cannot not cry. There is no simulation or synthesis of emotion; it just happens.

Oliver Tuhey
Beckenham

SIR – Seeing the contrast between Michael Vaughan's reactions to Ashes victory and his resignation, it is clear that he singularly failed to treat Kipling's two impostors just the same.

Alan Spriggs
Lymington

18 AUGUST 2008

SIR – Readers wishing to improve their hand-eye co-ordination should try catching flies in flight with one hand. When I played cricket I found this beneficial for fielding at first slip.

G.A. Baxter
Walton

29 AUGUST 2008

SIR – Reading Christopher Howse (Comment, 27 August) reminded me of an interview with Rachel Heyhoe-Flint, the then English cricket captain.

She was asked if they used an equivalent of the gentlemen's box.

'Oh yes,' she replied. 'We call them manhole covers.'

Robin Franklin
Heybridge Basin

2 SEPTEMBER 2008
'MANHOLE COVER' COINAGE

SIR – I blush at having such a 'Bernard Manning' type line attributed to this maiden of cricket (29 August).

The story is somewhat conveniently attached to my name, but the truth behind the creation is that I was batting for the England Women's XI versus An Old England XI at Chislehurst Common in 1963 with the dear late great Lord Cowdrey captaining his side. In the slips trying to 'sledge' me out were those two well known kings of cricket mirth, Peter Parfitt (Middlesex) and Peter Richardson (Kent). The former asked what protection women cricketers wear – and quick as a flash through the slips, Peter Richardson replied with the answer that I am too shy to repeat.

I must admit it made me giggle at the time. However, I stood firm and did not lose my wicket or my sense of humour.

Rachael Heyhoe Flint
Wolverhampton

28 NOVEMBER 2008

IT'S JUST NOT CRICKET

SIR – It's not only the Americans who are puzzled by our game of cricket. They can never understand how we can play the game for five days and get no clear result. What they would make of the fourth game in the one-day series in India, heaven knows. Both sides have 22 overs. The first side score 166 and the second side score 178 and yet the first side wins. Something called 'Duckworth-Lewis' apparently decides this.

Surely cricket has to find a simpler way of deciding the result of matches – and one that mere mortals can understand.

John Farrow
Harpenden

MADNESS IN METHOD

SIR – I can understand the annoyance of Kevin Pietersen re: the latest one-day international against India where England scored more runs than India but still lost. Can we rename it the Vera Duckworth method?

Colin Chegwyn
Launceston

THE EYES HAVE IT

SIR – I don't see why batsmen today accept being confronted by bowlers wearing gold necklaces and particularly sunglasses. When I played cricket no jewellery was worn. As batsmen, we liked to see the colour of the bowlers' eyes. Would an umpire uphold my complaint today if I refused to face a bowler so adorned?

Douglas J. Wathen
Rushford

CRICKET MUST BE SAVED FROM THE SHOUTING YOBS

SIR – Does Giles Clarke (5 August) not realise that he is trying to close the stable door after the horse has bolted? Rowdy behaviour at cricket matches should have been stamped out by the authorities years ago when the game was first hijacked by pot-bellied, beer-swilling, replica shirt-wearing football fans who only went to cricket matches for the all-day drinking.

Katy Cooke, the official spokeswoman for the Barmy Army, admits trying to get under the skin of an opposition player in order to cause him to lose concentration, but has she no respect for real cricket enthusiasts who go to Test matches in order to see some of the best players in the world?

This opportunity is being denied to them by Katy Cooke and her moronic friends. It is time the authorities stepped in and prevented a bunch of yobs ruining a once great sport.

Tony West
Panfield

26 AUGUST 2009

THE CRICKETING LEADERSHIP OF ANDREW STRAUSS

SIR – As one who has seen leadership under pressure at all levels, I would like to add my congratulations to Andrew Strauss. When he took over, English cricket was in crisis; he gave it inspiration and intelligent tactical direction.

Despite his extra responsibilities, he also enhanced his considerable batting skills and he never lost his head or his nerve when things started to go wrong.

He had some luck running for him at the Oval, but as Napoleon observed: 'Give me a lucky general.'

Altogether his intelligent leadership has been of the highest order by any standards. Success in the Ashes, although helped by some fine performances from his team, was largely a personal triumph for him. He is a man of character and courage whom others follow naturally.

Field Marshal Lord Bramall
London SW1

19 APRIL 2010

THE CRICKET BIBLE HAS PUBLISHED SWEAR WORDS BEFORE

SIR – Max Davidson reports on *Wisden*'s use of the f-word (Features, 15 April) as though it has never happened before. However, it (or a similar expletive) has appeared in three of the most recent five *Wisdens*. Not until Thursday had we received any communication of complaint. The total stands at one email.

The intention has never been to shock or cause offence, but to give a faithful and honest record of what major figures in the game have said.

All instances have been in direct quotations from players or

administrators, and on two occasions, the utterer of the expletive has received official censure.

Hugh Chevallier
Deputy Editor
Wisden Cricketers' Almanack
Alton

6 JULY 2010
TWENTY20 OVERKILL

SIR – As the cricket season plods on, with real cricket, which
produces Test players, replaced by Twenty20, which produces
money, I would like to know: 1) How many T20 games have
produced exciting finishes, and how many have been dead
contests before the end of the first innings? 2) What proportion
of income has been paid out to celebrity overseas cricketers
who have contributed little or nothing to the county they
represent? Would this money have been better spent trying to
produce young cricketers for the counties or for the England
team? 3) As many members of county clubs do not enjoy T20,
is there a danger that counties will lose income, as members
will not renew their membership next season?

Roy Woodcock
Malvern

31 AUGUST 2010
STILL CRICKET AT ITS BEST

SIR – If, as is alleged, touring cricketers contrived to see that
occurrences were decided in advance so as to inflict a scam on a
bookmaker mug enough to take a bet on what should have been
a remote possibility, and took money for setting this up, they may

be guilty of breaking a specific law and liable to prosecution.

If proven, such an action would certainly not be in the spirit nor indeed of the letter of the game, and it would be up to the cricket authorities, both national and international, to take the appropriate action to see such transgressions are not allowed to take root, just as the governing bodies in racing and other sports, where such things have been known to happen, have had to be continually on their guard.

It was most regrettable that this incident was alleged to have happened in the fourth Test between England and Pakistan at Lord's, the home of cricket. Let no one, however, try, as I am afraid some have tried to do, to consider this a significant part of the game itself, impinging on the historical reputation of this Test match.

The delivery of the odd obvious no-ball would not and did not change the course of the match or the outcome. Those of us privileged to be there saw two of the most interesting, fascinating and compelling days' cricket I can remember in a lifetime of being associated with the game.

On the second day, six wickets went down as a result of superb Pakistan bowling and two hundreds were put together as a result of concentrated application, at times brilliant, by two of England's batsmen. On the third day ten wickets were taken, largely due to excellent spin and swing bowling by England, with two 150s completed and records toppling all over the place.

Wickets falling, high-scoring innings and real tension between bat and ball – what more can one ask? It showed how Test cricket is the heart and soul of the game, and still is the most compelling viewing. It puts the transitory attractions of the Twenty20 game into the shade.

Field Marshal Lord Bramall
Ex-President MCC
Crondall
Hampshire

1 SEPTEMBER 2010

MONEY BEFORE CRICKET

SIR – Those cricket administrators who are keen to see the forthcoming one-day games between England and Pakistan go ahead are putting money ahead of the interests of the game. Sounds like match-fixing to me.

Andy Johnson
Camberley

SIR – There is a view that if no-balls are being used for illegal betting in cricket, then the overall result of a match is not affected. I'm afraid this is nonsense.

Take the last Test at Lord's. Let us assume the first no-ball bowled was to Trott when he was on 20. Had a legitimate delivery been bowled, it might well have dismissed him. As Trott eventually scored 184 in that innings, England would have compiled 164 runs fewer.

The runs scored by Broad then also come into the equation, as his partner for the whole of his innings was Trott. As there was only Anderson and Finn left to bat, it is highly unlikely that Broad would have scored more than about 30.

Their total for the innings would have been closer to 150 than the eventual 446 achieved. Despite Pakistan's low score of 74 in their innings, the follow-on would not have been an issue, so England would have to have batted for a second time.

The above is, of course, hypothetical: however, it does go to prove that the bowling of illegal no-balls can affect the outcome of a game.

Matthew Biddlecombe
Sampford Courtenay

SIR – We should congratulate the Pakistan cricketers for making an ancient, boring rain-making ceremony mildly interesting to a silent majority who probably could not name anyone in the English team.

Dr Ken Harvey
Trefecca

2 SEPTEMBER 2010
COUNTERFEIT CRICKET

SIR – Lord Bramall (31 August) seems content to watch a cricket match in which he cannot be sure that everything is above board.

Does he not feel in the slightest let down? If this type of scam is not dealt with vigorously then soon his Lordship will be sitting in half-empty grounds.

Ray Johnson
Hailsham

SIR – After years of allegations and whispers surrounding spot-fixing in cricket, what self-respecting bookie would take a bet on a specific event such as a no-ball or a dropped catch? The very nature of the bet reeks of corruption.

Damian Beeley
London SE24

3 SEPTEMBER 2010

SIR – One positive aspect to emerge from the shadows cast over cricket by the alleged events at Lord's is that the umpires correctly identified the no-balls in question. The foundations of the game of cricket, I believe, remain very solid.

Bob Ackroyd
Beaconsfield

18 SEPTEMBER 2010

SIR – If the Pope's presence at Westminster Abbey was seen as sufficient reason to interrupt BBC Radio 4's cricket commentary, could we invite him to stay here indefinitely?

David Gray
Richmond
North Yorkshire

11 OCTOBER 2010
SKITTLED IN THE PEW

SIR – Adults who seek an alternative to sermon bingo (8 October) should try sermon cricket. A histrionic preacher's gestures are similar to a cricket umpire's signals, and can be used to award boundaries, byes, no-balls, etc.

Choose likely words for singles and twos (e.g. Bible, sin) and a 'team' of 11 from church members, and you are ready to play. The raised finger, of course, is 'man out'.

An exciting result when I was a choirboy was delivered by a visiting preacher who stabbed his emphatic finger in the air ten times in the first three minutes, getting the whole team out for a duck.

The most unusual was a man whose heel became caught in the hem of his vestments. Lifting one knee as he raised his arm for emphasis, he managed to signal a leg bye.

Mik Shaw
Goring-by-Sea